FIFA WOMEN'S WORLD CUP
FRANCE 2019™

THE OFFICIAL BOOK

This edition published in 2019
by Carlton Books Limited
20 Mortimer Street, London W1T 3JW

A CIP catalogue record for this book is available from the British Library

ISBN 978-1-78739-216-8

Authors: Catherine Etoe, Jen O'Neill & Natalia Sollohub
Editorial Director: Martin Corteel
Managing Art Editor: Andri Johannsson
Design: Samantha Richiardi
Picture Research: Paul Langan
Production: Nicola Davey

Printed in Spain

Publisher's Note
The facts and records in
this book are accurate as
of 31 December 2018.

FIFA WOMEN'S WORLD CUP FRANCE 2019™

THE OFFICIAL BOOK

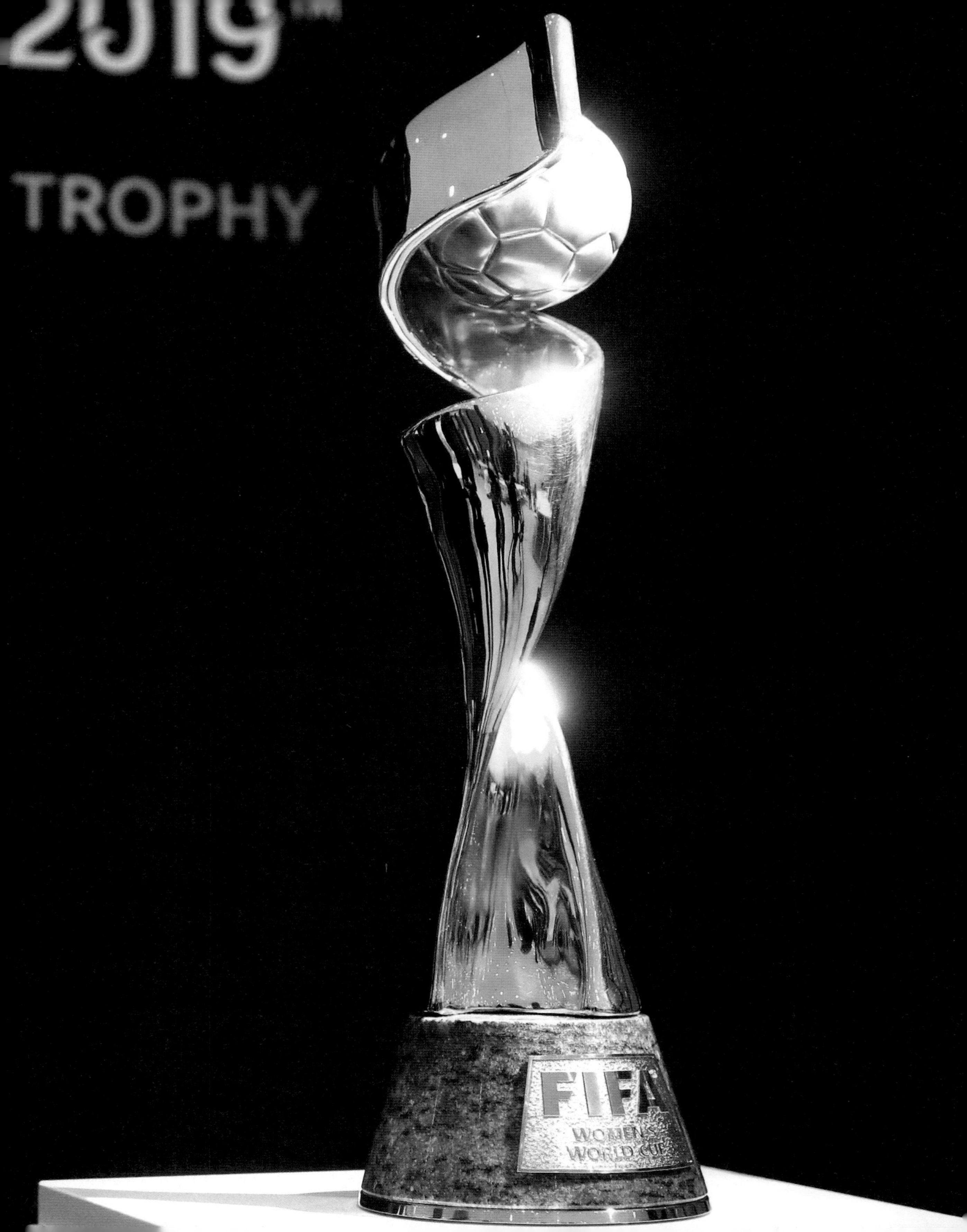
2019
TROPHY
FIFA
WOMEN'S
WORLD CUP

CONTENTS

CHAPTER 1:
WELCOME TO FRANCE — 8

DARE TO SHINE — 10

THE QUALIFYING TRAIL — 12

THE VENUES — 14

THE DRAW — 16

CHAPTER 2: — 18
ALLEZ LES BLEUES

HISTORY OF FRENCH — 20
WOMEN'S FOOTBALL

HEROINES OF FRENCH — 22
WOMEN'S FOOTBALL

FRENCH WOMEN'S FOOTBALL: — 24
KEY FACTS & STATS

CHAPTER 3: — 26
MEET THE TEAMS

GROUP A — 28

FRANCE — 30

KOREA REPUBLIC — 32

NORWAY — 34

NIGERIA — 36

GROUP B — 38

GERMANY — 40

CHINA PR — 42

SPAIN — 44

SOUTH AFRICA — 46

GROUP C — 48

AUSTRALIA — 50

ITALY — 52

BRAZIL — 54

JAMAICA — 56

GROUP D — 58

ENGLAND — 60

SCOTLAND — 62

ARGENTINA — 64

JAPAN — 66

GROUP E — 68

CANADA — 70

CAMEROON — 72

NEW ZEALAND — 74

THE NETHERLANDS — 76

GROUP F — 78

USA — 80

THAILAND — 82

CHILE — 84

SWEDEN — 86

CHAPTER 4: — 88
FIFA WOMEN'S WORLD CUP™ RECORDS

TEAM RECORDS — 90

PLAYER RECORDS — 92

MATCH SCHEDULE — 94

Opposite: The 47cm tall, gold-plated bronze and polished aluminium FIFA Women's World Cup trophy was designed in 1998. Since then it has been won twice by both Germany and the USA and once by Japan.

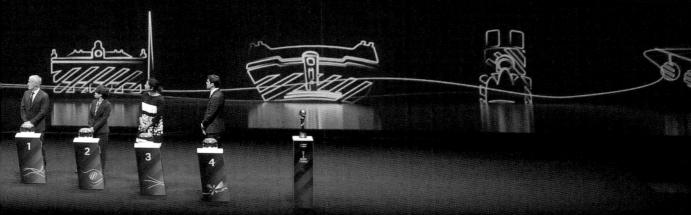

GROUP D

 ENGLAND

SCOTLAND

ARGENTINA

JAPAN

GROUP E

CANADA

CAMEROON

NEW ZEALAND

NETHERLANDS

GROUP F

 USA

THAILAND

CHILE

SWEDEN

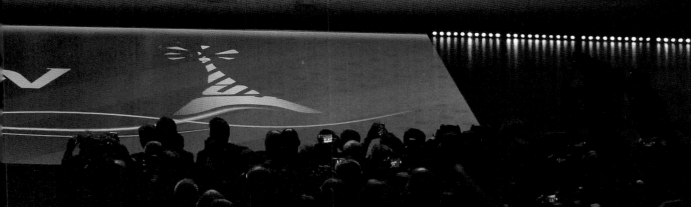

WELCOME TO FRANCE

Football fever hit France in 2018 as *Les Bleus* returned triumphantly from Russia having won the hallowed FIFA World Cup™ in some style. France has twice hosted the men's tournament and twice lifted the trophy. Now this magnificent country and its football-loving public welcome the prestigious FIFA Women's World Cup™. With 24 top teams set to play 52 games across nine charming cities, the stage is set for yet another memorable summer of football.

Main: *The globally recognised 324-metre tall Eiffel Tower dominates the skyline of Paris, the city that plays host to the tournament's opening fixture.*

DARE TO SHINE™

The challenge has been set for _Les Bleues_, the public and all visiting players and fans to light up the FIFA Women's World Cup™ this summer and the rallying cry is "Dare to Shine™".

THE TOURNAMENT'S official slogan captures the dual ambitions of those national sides competing for glory as well as the prospects for the sport in France and around the globe.

In short, a successful landmark event could dramatically boost the game's fortunes and the ambition is to see fuller stadiums and the biggest international television audience to date.

"We're looking for a billion TV viewers around the world and I am sure we will get them because women's football is growing fast," stated FIFA President Gianni Infantino at the tournament's ticket launch in Paris in September 2018.

Organisers also harbour ambitions that the tournament will create a social legacy by inspiring inclusivity and encouraging diversity, and one of their key missions is to be accessible to all, with affordable ticketing reflecting that aim.

"Our common goal is to make this event a family-oriented celebration for everyone," said France head coach Corinne Diacre.

France has previously held the UEFA European Women's U-18 and U-19 Championships (in 2000 and 2008 respectively) and the brilliantly received FIFA U-20 Women's World Cup 2018, in Brittany.

This will be the first time France has put on a senior women's competition though, and the prospect of becoming only the third European nation to host the world's biggest women's sporting event has captured the imagination of its national team stars.

Centre-back centurion Wendie Renard is certainly eager to emulate France men's famous triumph on home soil 21 years ago, a wish that is surely shared by her team-mates. "This is a dream come true to play a World Cup at home," she said. "We all remember 1998. I want to feel these emotions again."

Equally, the FIFA Women's World Cup is the ideal vehicle for the French Football Federation (FFF) to further its commitment to nurture and promote women's football as set out in its development plan in 2011.

Impressive gains have already been made over a relatively short period. The number of registered female players in France increased from 53,000 in 2011 to more than 125,000 by June 2018. An additional jump of 15 per cent in participation was recorded two months after the men's FIFA World Cup success in Russia.

If the women could follow in their footsteps, France would become the first nation to hold both the men's and women's trophies at the same time – and so the target of 200,000 by June 2019 appears an achievable one.

A decade ago, _Les Bleues_ were not major contenders on the international stage, having fared no better than ninth at their single appearance at a FIFA Women's World Cup in 2003. Now they are one of the most consistently exciting, technically pleasing and entertaining teams in the world. By 2018, French sides had also featured in all but one of the UEFA Women's Champions

League finals this decade, Olympique Lyonnais being victorious in five of the seven finals they had played in.

France have fallen at the knockout stage in five major tournaments since their brilliant run to the FIFA Women's World Cup semi-finals in 2011 was ended by the USA. Where better to make an historic mark in 2019 than in front of their own fans?

France's former star defender Laura Georges, who played in three FIFA Women's World Cup final tournaments and is now General Secretary of the FFF, believes that _Les Bleues_ should be bold. "We have been frustrated for many years, being so close to winning something," she said. "Everyone has said that France should win something so maybe it's time. Let's see!"

Of course, all the teams on the pitch this summer will "Dare to Shine" – the question is, who will shine brightest at the FIFA Women's World Cup 2019?

**Below:** Former France defender Sabrina Delannoy and Vice-President of the FFF Brigitte Henriques pose in Paris with the FIFA Women's World Cup 2019 official mascot, "ettie".

THE QUALIFYING TRAIL

Four first-timers are set to join the hosts, seven ever-present sides and 12 other teams to fight for footballing glory this summer.

NEWCOMERS Chile, Jamaica, Scotland and South Africa will come together with leading lights including Brazil, Germany, Japan, Nigeria, Norway, Sweden and the USA, who have all featured at every edition of the FIFA Women's World Cup™.

The road to France began in the spring of 2017 and reached a dramatic climax in winter 2018 having traversed six continents. From the world's most populous countries China and India, to some of the smallest islands on the planet, 140 teams entered the mix and thousands of players proudly wore their nation's colours as they dared to dream of reaching the FIFA Women's World Cup France 2019.

The quest kicked off on 3 April 2017 with eight matches in the AFC Asian qualifying preliminary round. Twelve months on, the AFC Women's Asian Cup in Jordan produced the first side, other than hosts France, to book their ticket to the finals when China PR topped their group to take one of the five available slots. They were swiftly joined by Asian heavyweights Japan and Australia, along with Thailand and the winners of the fifth place play-off, Korea Republic.

At the *Copa América Femenina* 2018, also in April, Brazil comfortably clinched their seventh South American title and secured an eighth successive FIFA Women's World Cup appearance, while hosts Chile put in a tremendous effort to beat Argentina,

Opposite: USA striker Alex Morgan netted 18 goals in 19 international games in a stellar 2018. She also won the Golden Boot as top scorer at the Concacaf Women's Championship in qualifying.

finish as runners-up and take the other automatic place. All was not lost for *La Albiceleste*, however. After a seven-month wait, they faced the fourth-placed side from Concacaf and a 5-1 win over two legs against Panama confirmed their eventual qualification for France 2019.

Just days after the earliest action had commenced in Asia, European sides began competing in their preliminary phase too. By far the busiest confederation, UEFA qualifying featured 46 teams taking part in 170 matches. During the year-long main group stage from September 2017 onwards, teams faced each other home and away, with only the seven table-toppers automatically assured a place at the finals.

First to make it through were Spain and then Italy, both on 8 June. The Spanish did not drop a single point during their impressive campaign and were home and dry with two games to spare. They were followed in August and September by England and then Germany, Norway, Scotland and Sweden, who had all been pushed more closely and won crunch ties to ensure their passage to France.

That left the four best runners-up to battle it out for the one remaining coveted berth in a mini play-off tournament and it was the Netherlands, the UEFA Women's EURO 2017 champions, who had the nerve and firepower to prevail. They beat Denmark twice and then Switzerland 4-1 on aggregate over two legs, to make it to their second successive finals.

Current world champions the USA continued their dominance

at October's Concacaf Women's Championship and will be joined in June by runners-up Canada and history-makers Jamaica. The Caribbean's first-ever qualifiers put paid to Panama in a penalty shoot-out after a 2-2 deadlock to snatch a spot in France.

With the December draw fast approaching, Nigeria defended their continental crown at the Women's Africa Cup of Nations in Ghana but they required two successive penalty shoot-out victories to do so. Those wins came against fellow qualifiers Cameroon in the semi-finals and South Africa in the final.

Last but not least was Oceania. Clear favourites, New Zealand's *Football Ferns* did not disappoint, with 43 goals scored and none conceded on their way to lifting the OFC Women's Nations Cup.

The qualifying trail involved 20 months of competition and 388 matches, but the race to be the best will not end until 7 July. Who will last the distance at the FIFA Women's World Cup 2019?

Below: The Netherlands navigated their way through the pressure of the UEFA play-offs to secure the final European place at France 2019.

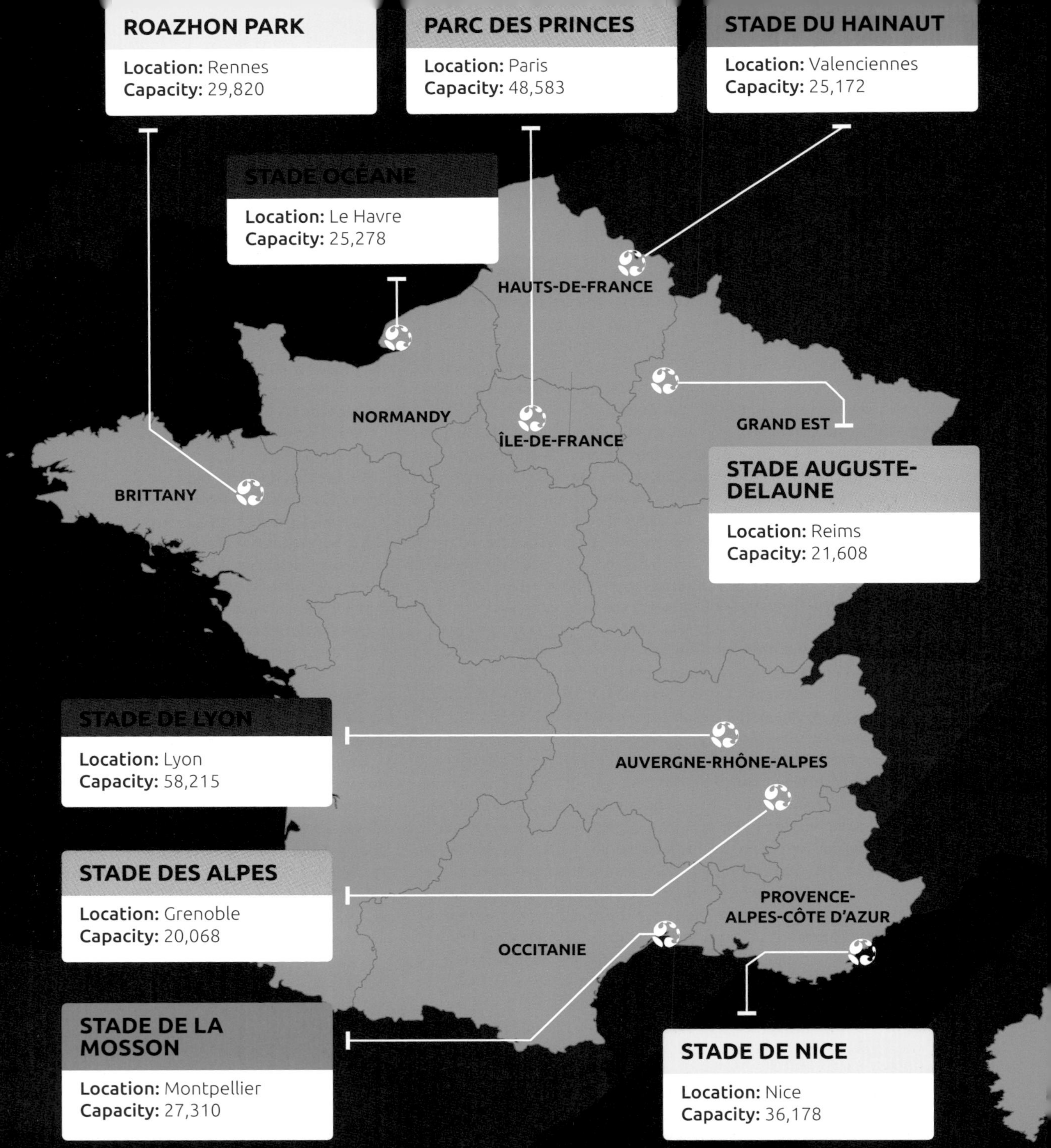

ROAZHON PARK

Location: Rennes
Capacity: 29,820

PARC DES PRINCES

Location: Paris
Capacity: 48,583

STADE DU HAINAUT

Location: Valenciennes
Capacity: 25,172

STADE OCÉANE

Location: Le Havre
Capacity: 25,278

HAUTS-DE-FRANCE

NORMANDY

ÎLE-DE-FRANCE

GRAND EST

BRITTANY

STADE AUGUSTE-DELAUNE

Location: Reims
Capacity: 21,608

STADE DE LYON

Location: Lyon
Capacity: 58,215

AUVERGNE-RHÔNE-ALPES

STADE DES ALPES

Location: Grenoble
Capacity: 20,068

PROVENCE-ALPES-CÔTE D'AZUR

OCCITANIE

STADE DE LA MOSSON

Location: Montpellier
Capacity: 27,310

STADE DE NICE

Location: Nice
Capacity: 36,178

THE VENUES

———— //// ————

A football-loving country famed as a centre of culture, philosophy and fine cuisine, France has vast experience of hosting world-class sporting events. Having twice played proud host to the men's event, now it will extend its *joie de vivre* to the FIFA Women's World Cup 2019™.

THE NINE VENUE CITIES will offer fans, visiting teams and dignitaries a hugely enriching experience and the chance to explore France, one of the most popular tourist destinations on the planet. From the footballing hotbed of the north and the romantic ambience of the capital, via the wine regions of the Rhône Valley and the beauty of the Alps to the sunshine and coastline of the Riviera, the locations of the magnificent stadiums that play host to this tournament will reflect the nation's varied geography, accents and flavours.

What better place to kick off a celebration of women's football than in Paris, the City of Light? On the evening of Friday, 7 June, Paris Saint-Germain's beautifully modernised Parc des Princes will be the setting for the opening game, ensuring that match-goers enjoy a first-rate experience in the stands as well as world-class football on the field.

The group-stage and round-of-16 action spans out across the nation, taking in Valenciennes, Le Havre, Reims, Paris, Rennes, Grenoble, Nice and Montpellier.

The most northerly venue, Valenciennes is just 15km from the Belgian border and within reasonable travel distance from European capitals Paris, Brussels, Amsterdam, London and Luxembourg City. The Normandy seaport of Le Havre boasts a Blue Flag beach, its city centre is a UNESCO World Heritage Site and Le Havre Athletic Club is the oldest football and rugby club in France. Reims is known as the City of Kings for its central role in French history and its club Stade de Reims has a revered past as two-time European Cup runners-up to Real Madrid in the 1950s. They also play at one of the tournament's smallest venues. Similarly compact, Grenoble's Stade des Alpes has a stunning mountainous backdrop and holds just over 20,000, but the city itself is the largest in the Alpine region. Renowned for its winter sports and local team Grenoble Foot 38, it is an important site in terms of history, art and scientific research. Situated near to the Mediterranean and boasting a sun-drenched and dry

climate is the thriving hotspot of Montpellier; while Rennes in Brittany, the region that put on the FIFA U-20 Women's World Cup 2018, with its pretty medieval centre, hosts the last quarter-final before the focus shifts southwards.

Residents of Nice – the cultural and economic capital of the Côte d'Azur – are rightly proud of their Promenade des Anglais and the city's many attractions, elegantly positioned between the grandeur of the Alps and the beautiful blue sea. Their new stadium, built for local club OGC Nice in 2013, will host the play-off for third place.

Capital of Gaul during the time of the Roman Empire and now home to France and Europe's most successful women's club side (in 2018 Olympique Lyonnais lifted the UEFA Women's Champions League trophy for a record fifth time), Lyon is the country's second largest metropolitan area. Lyon is also the place to see the semi-finals and final of the most prestigious competition in the women's game. Opened in 2016, the third largest and one of the most modern stadiums in France, Stade de Lyon can seat more than 58,000 spectators. Between fixtures, visitors will have time to savour the sights and tastes of this artistic and gastronomic centre.

All 52 matches will be played on natural grass, news surely welcomed by traditionalists after Canada 2015 was the first senior FIFA tournament to use FIFA-recommended 2-star football turf for every fixture. The scene is set. *Bienvenue en France.*

THE DRAW

Some of the biggest names in the world of football assembled at La Seine Musicale in Paris on 8 December 2018 for the moment 24 national teams and their supporters had been waiting for, the Draw for the FIFA Women's World Cup France 2019™.

JOINED BY AN international TV audience, the 2,000 officials, coaches, media and fans gathered in the auditorium were treated to a fantastical show of silhouetted dancers moving to form shapes representing the nine Host Cities, but once USA captain Carli Lloyd brought the trophy onto the stage, it was time to get down to the business in hand.

With male and female "FIFA Legends" such as Cindy Cone, Didier Deschamps, Michael Essien, Steffi Jones and Aya Miyama drawing the balls and fellow former international stars Alex Scott and Louis Saha overseeing proceedings, the make-up of the six groups gradually emerged.

France and the five other top seeds filled Pot 1, while the placement of the remaining 18 sides was determined by the FIFA Women's World Ranking. One of the most highly anticipated fixtures was, of course, the opening match. With the hosts automatically assigned first position in Group A, the honour has fallen to Korea Republic to kick off against France at the Parc des Princes in Paris, on the evening of 7 June. The two nations first met at USA 2003, when Marinette Pichon's strike ensured a 1-0 victory for *Les Bleues*.

Current holders the USA will commence their defence of the trophy against comparative newcomers Thailand in Group F. They are also joined by perennial finals opponents Sweden, making this a record fifth tournament in a row in which the two sides will meet and the sixth time in total. Their showdown could decide who advances as group winners and will conclude the group phase.

A sense of déjà vu pervades other line-ups too, with Group E containing familiar foes. Canada, Oceania champions New Zealand and the Netherlands all met in group play four years ago. The higher-ranked *Canucks* drew both games while the Dutch beat the *Football Ferns* 1-0. Having since won UEFA Women's EURO 2017, expect the *Oranje Leeuwinnen* to be an even tougher prospect this time around.

Group D could stand for "drama", with a tasty opening encounter in store between England and their neighbours Scotland. This will also be the fourth consecutive FIFA Women's World Cup in which the *Lionesses* have run into Japan. Both sides will hope to have qualified when they meet in their third game but fresh in the mind will be the stoppage-time defeat England suffered to the *Nadeshiko* in the semi-finals in 2015.

Several other intriguing combinations complete the draw, with diverse styles from four different continents brought together in Group C. Top seeds Australia will come up against Europeans Italy, before facing South American champions Brazil and first-ever Caribbean qualifiers Jamaica.

Meanwhile Group B features twice winners and current Olympic champions Germany, who will be looking to return to the top under new boss Martina Voss-Tecklenburg. However, they must first overcome China PR, debutants South Africa and tournament dark horses Spain.

Opposite: Captain of the defending champions the USA, Carli Lloyd, carries the FIFA Women's World Cup trophy onto the stage to mark the beginning of the draw.

Above: World Cup winners Didier Deschamps and Aya Miyama delight in the draw.

ALLEZ
LES BLEUES

The French women's domestic league and national team, respected and appreciated around the world, owe much to the legends and patrons of the past. From pioneers of the early 20th century such as Alice Milliat to stalwarts of the modern era like coaching legend Élisabeth Loisel, striking star Marinette Pichon and standard-bearer Sandrine Soubeyrand, all have played their part, setting records, breaking new ground and inspiring future generations. This is their story.

Main: Record goalscorer Marinette Pichon (number 9) and her France team-mates celebrate a goal against Italy in 2005, one of 81 she netted for Les Bleues.

HISTORY OF FRENCH WOMEN'S FOOTBALL

TODAY, THE FRENCH domestic league is considered one of the best in the world and the country's national team has earned the right to be viewed in the same light. It has taken many years to get to this point and if we turn the pages of history back 100 years, we see women's footballers coming together in the earliest competitive teams, facing their rivals in a league championship and travelling overseas together as the first national side.

Paris was a hotbed of the organised game in those early days, with teams such as Femina Sport, En Avant and Les Sportives de Paris breaking new ground as they competed for honours in a football championship and French cup competition organised by the *Fédération des sociétés féminines sportives de France* (FSFSF).

Wearing the colours of their homeland, players from these clubs made further inroads in 1920 when they came together as an FSFSF-select "France" to play England's most famous team of the era, Dick, Kerr Ladies. These two stylish teams played in front of thousands on that maiden tour of England and again in the return fixtures later that year in Paris, Roubaix, Le Havre and Rouen.

Even though The Football Association banned women from playing on their affiliated grounds in 1921, French sides would cross the Channel for matches many more times in the years that

Above: *Jessica Houara (8), captain Wendie Renard (2) and Eugénie Le Sommer (9) acknowledge the crowd at the FIFA Women's World Cup Canada 2015.*

Above: Current France head coach Corinne Diacre captained the side at their first FIFA Women's World Cup in the USA in 2003.

followed. This unique alliance and the women's game in France were halted by the outbreak of the Second World War and a subsequent ban on females playing football by the wartime regime.

In the decade after the end of the war, "France" – thought to be made up of players from across the country – took on "England" represented by Preston Ladies (formerly Dick, Kerr's) once again. It was, however, not until the late 1960s that French women footballers truly emerged from the shadows, helped in no small part by champions of the game such as journalist and coach Pierre Geoffroy who helped create a women's team at Stade de Reims and was the first coach of a new national side.

On 29 March 1970, official recognition of the women's game by the French Football Federation (FFF) finally arrived. The following year, France and the Netherlands faced each other in Hazebrouck in a game that would become the first FIFA recognised women's international. That season, more than 2,000 women were registered to play and in 1974 they were able to do so in an FFF-organised 16-team French Women's Championship.

Geoffroy's Reims dominated the early years of that elite league, winning five of the first eight titles. Since then, teams including VGA Saint-Maur and FCF Juvisy have also been victors on multiple occasions, although none can match the might of Lyon. Formed in 1970 as FCF Lyon, they were taken over by Olympique Lyonnais in 2004 and in 2018 they were crowned national champions for the 16th time and UEFA Women's Champions League winners for a record fifth.

Having attracted major overseas signings, such as the USA's Megan Rapinoe and Sweden's Lotta Schelin while nurturing French talent such as Laura Georges, Amandine Henry, Amel Majri, Louisa Nécib-Cadamuro and Wendie Renard over the years, this professional outfit has become the leading light at home and abroad.

Looking ahead to this summer's FIFA Women's World Cup™, it is safe to say that the French national set-up has sought to carve out a similar reputation, but it has taken time. With one solitary run to a two-legged quarter-final in 1988 under their belt, France did not qualify for a UEFA Women's Championship final tournament until 1997 and it is only in the last decade that they have reached the knockout stage again, returning home after the quarter-finals for the past three editions, twice following penalty shoot-out defeats.

As for the FIFA Women's World Cup, France did not qualify until 2003 and missed out in 2007, but were fourth at Germany 2011 under former head coach Bruno Bini. It says much for their development that they were disappointed to only reach the quarter-finals at Canada 2015 with Philippe Bergeroô. After all, since finishing in the top four of their first Women's Olympic Football Tournament in 2012, France have been ranked one of the top six teams in the world.

HEROINES OF FRENCH WOMEN'S FOOTBALL

France has produced its fair share of footballing heroines down the years. From the early pioneers of a hundred years ago to the stars of the recent past, these women have inspired generations with their determination, spirit and landmark achievements while laying the groundwork for the game we now know.

Above: *The French and English team captains kiss on the cheek and shake hands before kick-off in a 1925 friendly match.*

THOSE WHO played in the days before 1970 when women's football was officially recognised in France are all heroines in their own right. Of special mention, though, are Thérèse Brulé and Suzanne Liébrard of Femina Sport club and Alice Milliat, president of the *Fédération des sociétés féminines sportives de France* (FSFSF). Brulé and Liébrard were the captains of the two teams in the first women's match on French soil in 1917 and it was on Milliat's watch that the FSFSF introduced football championships for women. Milliat also led the first "France" team on their maiden overseas tour in 1920. Various French teams would go on to play overseas throughout the next two decades, and Femina star Carmen Pomiès even ran out for English works team Dick, Kerr Ladies in the early 1920s. Together, these secretaries, dressmakers, dentists, champion athletes and sports enthusiasts flew the *tricolore* with pride.

Blazing a trail several decades later was Élisabeth Loisel, the first head coach to lead France to a FIFA Women's World Cup™. Kicking off as a child with US Etrepilly in

Above: *France forward and legend Marinette Pichon jumps for joy after scoring against Brazil at the FIFA Women's World Cup 2003.*

two FIFA Women's World Cups, five UEFA Women's EURO tournaments and an Olympic Games, she was just two appearances shy of a double century when she retired in 2013. She is also a legend at FCF Juvisy where she spent most of her career, winning two French league titles and the French Cup before hanging up her boots aged 40.

Marinette Pichon is another player to have surpassed the achievements of many other national team footballers, both male and female. A clinical finisher, she debuted for France in 1994 and, upon her retirement in 2007 at the age of 31, had netted a record 81 goals in 112 appearances.

Like those early pioneers, Pichon also flew the flag for France abroad as the first Frenchwoman to play professionally in the USA. In a stellar two seasons with Women's United Soccer Association (WUSA) league side Philadelphia Charge, she was crowned best forward and the WUSA's most valuable player of 2002 and top scorer of 2003. Selected for the World Stars team that played at the Stade de France to celebrate FIFA's centenary in 2004, she also went down in history as the scorer of France's first goal at a FIFA Women's World Cup.

Starring alongside Pichon, Soubeyrand, Bompastor and Georges at that tournament in 2003 was former defender and current France head coach Corinne Diacre. Already an inspiration to many after being capped 121 times by France, she also boasts the distinction of being the first woman to coach a professional men's team in the French league.

As France 2019 dawns, Diacre will walk in her former manager Loisel's ground-breaking footsteps, while her charges will follow in those of their nation's greatest modern-day players. As ever in football, though, they will no doubt be looking to make a little history of their own.

1970, the year that the French Football Federation (FFF) officially recognised the women's game, Loisel retired aged 26 with 41 France caps and seven French titles to her name, one won as player-coach of VGA Saint-Maur.

For the next 18 years, Loisel helped shape the women's game in France, both through her work as FFF national organiser and as head coach. During her tenure, France qualified for three major tournaments and the FFF set up a national female academy at Clairefontaine to bring through the country's best young players. Among the early graduates from the CNFE Clairefontaine academy are

recently retired internationals such as Camille Abily, an ambassador at the FIFA U-20 Women's World Cup 2018 in France, and Laura Georges, another inspiration to footballers of the future through her work as FFF General Secretary. Fellow international retirees Sonia Bompastor, Louisa Nécib-Cadamuro and Élodie Thomis are also CNFE graduates. All role models in their own right, this group boast more than 800 appearances for *Les Bleues* between them.

The most capped footballer in France male or female is, however, former midfielder and captain Sandrine Soubeyrand. A key member of the French squad for

FRENCH WOMEN'S FOOTBALL: KEY FACTS & STATS

WOMEN HAVE played organised football in France for over a century but it was not until 1970 that the French Football Federation first registered female players. The national team's inaugural match under their auspices took place the following year and has since been recognised by FIFA as the first official women's international.

Above: Sandrine Soubeyrand, France's most-capped player.

DID YOU KNOW...?

When Sandrine Soubeyrand broke Lilian Thuram's record of 142 *Équipe de France* appearances in 2009, he presented her with a framed "143" shirt on the pitch in front of 9,500 spectators in Le Havre.

RECORDS UNDER THE FRENCH FOOTBALL FEDERATION

First international match
| France 4-0 The Netherlands | Friendly | 17 Apr 1971 |

First competitive match
| France 1-0 Italy | EURO qualifier | 30 Oct 1982 |

First appearance in a knockout tie
| Italy 2-0 France | EURO quarter-final 1st leg | 27 Nov 1988 |

First UEFA Women's EURO finals appearance
Norway/Sweden 1997

First FIFA Women's World Cup™ finals appearance
USA 2003

First Olympic Games appearance
London 2012

First goal
| Jocelyne Ratignier v The Netherlands | 17 Apr 1971 |

First hat-trick
| Jocelyne Ratignier v The Netherlands | 17 Apr 1971 |

First competitive goal
| Isabelle Musset v Italy | EURO qualifier | 30 Oct 1982 |

First goal at a UEFA Women's EURO
| Angélique Roujas v Spain | 29 Jun 1997 |

First goal at a FIFA Women's World Cup
| Marinette Pichon v Korea Republic | 24 Sep 2003 |

First goal at an Olympic Games
| Gaëtane Thiney v USA | 25 Jul 2012 |

Record victory in a friendly
| France 14-0 Algeria | 14 May 1998 |

Record competitive victory
| France 14-0 Bulgaria | WWC qualifier | 28 Nov 2013 |

Record defeat in a friendly
| Germany 7-0 France | 2 Sep 1992 |

Record competitive defeat
| Germany 5-1 France | EURO group match | 27 Aug 2009 |

Longest winning run
| 17 matches | Aug 2011 – Jul 2012 |

Longest unbeaten run
| 19 matches | Jul 2013 – Jun 2014 |

| Highest FIFA Women's World Ranking | 3rd |
| Lowest FIFA Women's World Ranking | 10th |

RECORD GOALSCORER:
Marinette Pichon

- Scored 81 goals in 112 appearances for France.
- Netted in the play-off final win over England that saw France qualify for their first FIFA Women's World Cup finals.
- Scored France's first FIFA Women's World Cup goal in 2003 v Korea Republic.
- Retired from international football after the draw with England in Rennes that saw the visitors pip France to China 2007.

RECORD CAP HOLDER:
Sandrine Soubeyrand

- Represented her country 198 times, captaining the side for six years.
- Led France at four major tournaments: UEFA Women's EURO 2009, FIFA Women's World Cup 2011, London 2012 Olympic Games, UEFA Women's EURO 2013.
- Retired from the national team after Denmark knocked France out on penalties in the quarter-finals of UEFA Women's EURO 2013.
- Presented with the honour of *Chevalier de l'Ordre National du Mérite* in 2013.

France at UEFA finals

- Played in every UEFA Women's EURO finals since the introduction of a group stage in 1997: three group-stage exits and three quarter-final finishes.
- Also appeared in a two-legged quarter-final in 1988, losing 4-1 on aggregate to Italy.
- Winners of UEFA Women's Under-19 EURO four times.
- Runners-up three times at the UEFA Women's Under-17 EURO.

France at FIFA finals

- Three FIFA Women's World Cup finals appearances: group stage in 2003; fourth place in 2011; quarter-finalists in 2015.
- Two Olympic Games appearances: fourth place in 2012; quarter-finalists in 2016.
- Winners: FIFA U-17 Women's World Cup Azerbaijan 2012.
- Runners-up: FIFA U-20 Women's World Cup Papua New Guinea 2016.

Above: Wendie Renard raises the SheBelieves Cup trophy, 2017.

DID YOU KNOW...?

France's longest unbeaten run against one particular nation lasted nearly 43 years. England had beaten their neighbours in their first two meetings, in 1973 and 1974, but had to wait more than four decades before triumphing again, 1-0 in the UEFA Women's EURO 2017 quarter-finals, after 19 matches without a victory.

BEST SHOWING AT INTERNATIONAL TOURNAMENTS

FIFA Women's World Cup	Fourth place: 2011
Olympic Games	Fourth place: 2012
UEFA Women's EURO	Quarter-finalists: 1988, 2009, 2013, 2017
Algarve Cup	Runners-up: 2015
Cyprus Cup	Winners: 2012, 2014
SheBelieves Cup	Winners: 2017

DID YOU KNOW...?

Les Bleues went unbeaten throughout their whole UEFA Women's EURO 2013 campaign, winning all of their qualification games, as well as the group matches at the finals in Sweden, only to go out on penalties after drawing with Denmark in the quarter-finals.

HEAD COACHES UNDER THE FFF

Pierre Geoffroy	1971-1978	17 matches
Francis-Pierre Coché	1978-1987	35 matches
Aimé Mignot	1987-1997	79 matches
Élisabeth Loisel	1997-2007	114 matches
Bruno Bini	2007-2013	98 matches
Philippe Bergerôo	2013-2016	55 matches
Olivier Echouafni	2016-2017	15 matches
Corinne Diacre	September 2017-	

MEET THE TEAMS

It takes tenacity and talent to reach the pinnacle of any sport and you can be sure that the elite female footballers who run out at this FIFA Women's World Cup™ – be they ambitious debutants, experienced campaigners or tournament favourites – will relish this opportunity to shine in front of a worldwide audience. The hard-fought qualification campaigns are over, the time to perform on the world stage is finally here. Let's meet the 24 teams.

Below: The USA avenged their FIFA Women's World Cup 2011 final shoot-out defeat to Japan by blowing their opponents away in a 5-2 victory to lift the trophy in Vancouver four years later.

GROUP A

All eyes will be on the Parc des Princes, Paris on 7 June as France face Korea Republic in the tournament opener. The hosts' all-European clash with 1995 winners Norway in Nice could be a group decider, while African powerhouses Nigeria will pose a challenge to any opposition.

Main: The opening match of the tournament will be played at the Parc des Princes in Paris. The fifth largest stadium in the country, it was the home of the French football and rugby national teams until the Stade de France was opened in 1998.

 FRANCE

Will the host nation dare to shine?

As hosts, France were always certain of their place at this summer's FIFA Women's World Cup™, but the heat is on *Les Bleues* to deliver in the wake of their men's success at Russia 2018.

THE COACH

CORINNE DIACRE
An inspirational former defender, Diacre joined ASJ Soyaux aged 14 and debuted for France at 18 in 1993, going on to captain her country and play in four major tournaments. France's first female centurion, she retired in 2005 with 121 caps. Picked for the FIFA World Stars team in 1999 and in 2002 scored against England in a European play-off to send France to their maiden FIFA Women's World Cup. A calm, no-nonsense coach known for her attention to detail, she honed her skills at Soyaux, as France assistant coach and then as manager of men's *Ligue 2* professional side Clermont Foot for three seasons.

Above: More than four years after they were awarded the tournament, the French team will be ready to play.

KICKING OFF the tournament at the Parc des Princes on 7 June will be France's first hurdle, but it should not be a baptism of fire. For although France have not faced the rigours of qualification, they have undergone intense preparation in front of thousands of fans.

The kickstart in their readiness for this summer's tournament came in March 2018 in the wake of a shock 4-1 loss to England in the four-nation SheBelieves Cup in the USA. France rallied to draw 1-1 with USA and beat Germany 3-0, but in the aftermath head coach Corinne Diacre decided to get back to basics.

Rather than concentrate on results, France focused on the development of a sturdy defensive line, swifter transition into attack, an improved goal ratio and a desire to inspire home fans to become

what Diacre described as their 12th woman.

Within seven months they had overturned Nigeria, Canada, Mexico, Australia and Cameroon, scoring 21 and conceding none. Watched by a total of around 45,000 spectators in stadiums across the country, the friendlies were a showcase for the home side.

They were also a testing ground as Diacre, at the helm since September 2017, sought to create a squad capable of going beyond France's FIFA Women's World Cup best-ever finish of fourth in 2011, when she was assistant to then head coach Bruno Bini.

With so many of that generation recently retired, it was no simple task but stalwarts Sarah Bouhaddi, Wendie Renard, Élise Bussaglia, Eugénie Le Sommer and Gaëtane

AMEL MAJRI
Born: 25 January 1993
Position: Defender/Midfielder

Born in Tunisia but raised in France, this talented footballer could have played for either nation, but *Les Bleues* won out. Boasts a sweet left foot, crowd-pleasing ball skills, seemingly limitless energy and is super experienced after 12 years with leading French side Olympique Lyonnais. Domestic and European champion at the age of 18, she debuted for France three years later. Already has games for the national team at the FIFA Women's World Cup 2015 and the 2016 Olympics under her belt, and at 26 is still to hit her peak.

AMANDINE HENRY
Born: 28 September 1989
Position: Midfielder

Awarded the adidas Silver Ball at the FIFA Women's World Cup 2015, with her wonder goal against Mexico winning admirers across the globe. Made the first FIFA/FIFPro Women's World XI the following year. Then joined Portland Thorns in the USA to challenge herself after winning multiple trophies with Olympique Lyonnais. Returned home in 2017 with National Women's Soccer League shield and championship winners medals. Combative, un-showy but skilful and has proved a more than capable captain of her country.

EUGÉNIE LE SOMMER
Born: 18 May 1989
Position: Forward

Crowned French National Union of Professional Footballers women's player of 2010 and 2015 and has won every domestic trophy and the UEFA Women's Champions League multiple times with Olympique Lyonnais. One of nine children with a mother who also played football, she passed the 150-cap mark with France at the SheBelieves Cup in 2018 and was prolific in the build-up to this summer's tournament. A big game player, she boasts a ratio of a goal every two games and adds flair and experience to France's frontline.

Above: The team's captain and midfield engine room, Amandine Henry.

WOMEN'S WORLD CUP RECORD

Year	Venue	Result
1991	China PR	Did not qualify
1995	Sweden	Did not qualify
1999	USA	Did not qualify
2003	USA	Group stage (3rd, Group B)
2007	China PR	Did not qualify
2011	Germany	Fourth place
2015	Canada	Quarter-finalists

Thiney have come to the fore. Coming of age too are the versatile Amel Majri plus FIFA Women's World Cup youth medallists such as Griedge Mbock Bathy, Kadidiatou Diani and Grace Geyoro.

Since 2013, France have reached the knockout stage of four consecutive major tournaments only to lose in the quarter-finals. Remarkably, their internationally respected head coach ended her playing days trophyless. Maybe, with fresh faces and fulsome home support, 2019 will be their year.

KOREA REPUBLIC

Rising stars of the east set to give it their all

The *Taeguk Ladies* were the toast of their nation when they returned home having reached the last 16 of the FIFA Women's World Cup 2015™. Can this determined squad make heads turn again four years on?

Above: Already through to the FIFA Women's World Cup, Korea Republic also celebrated a third-place finish in the Asian Games in August 2018.

WITH A modern-day national set-up that is barely 30 years old and a domestic league that was founded only a decade ago, Korea Republic will be one of the younger women's football nations on show this summer. Even so, with their flair, defensive strength and goalscoring prowess, the *Taeguk Ladies* will be formidable opponents.

Yoon Deok-yeo's side certainly gave a few top nations a run for their money in qualifying and the banner that was draped over the stands as they celebrated their achievement in April 2018 summed up their campaign perfectly. "Korea! Just Go For It!" it read, and it is fair to say that they had done precisely that.

First off, they had to pip Korea DPR to a place at the 19th AFC Women's Asian Cup, the tournament whose five best finishers would qualify for France 2019. Their journey almost ended at the preliminary stage in Pyongyang when they fell a goal down in front of over 40,000 spectators, but Jang Sel-gi pulled it back to 1-1. That precious point combined with high-scoring wins over India, Hong Kong and Uzbekistan, was enough to see them through to the tournament proper on goal difference.

When the AFC Women's Asian Cup kicked off a year later, Korea Republic held top sides Australia and Japan to goalless draws

CHO SO-HYUN

Born: 24 June 1988
Position: Midfielder

A calm and inspirational skipper who came to the sport late but has made up for lost time and now boasts over 115 caps. Loves the big occasion, bosses the national team from central midfield and can pop up with crucial goals. Eager to challenge herself, she became the first woman from Korea Republic to sign for a Norwegian side when she joined Avaldsnes in 2018 after playing on loan in Japan with INAC Kobe Leonessa. Joined English club West Ham United in January 2019.

JI SO-YUN

Born: 21 February 1991
Position: Midfielder

The *Taeguk Ladies'* youngest-ever goalscorer – having opened her account aged 15 – and now their all-time top scorer. Thrilling to watch with her clever runs and fine control, her ability to play in midfield or leading the line is an asset for both club and country. A genuine role model at home and abroad, she is a definite fans' favourite at Chelsea in England too, where she has won multiple league titles and the hallowed Women's FA Cup.

LEE MIN-A

Born: 8 November 1991
Position: Midfielder/Forward

A livewire with the vision to bring her team-mates into play, she shone at two youth-level FIFA Women's World Cups before making her senior international debut in 2012. Now a regular starter, she was joint-top scorer for her country at the AFC Women's Asian Cup 2018. Crowned KFA Women's Footballer of the Year in 2017, she won five consecutive WK League titles with Incheon Hyundai Steel before making the leap overseas to join INAC Kobe Leonessa in January 2018.

WOMEN'S WORLD CUP RECORD

Year	Venue	Result
1991	China PR	Did not qualify
1995	Sweden	Did not qualify
1999	USA	Did not qualify
2003	USA	Group stage (4th Group B)
2007	China PR	Did not qualify
2011	Germany	Did not qualify
2015	Canada	Round of 16

but missed out on automatic qualification and the semi-finals on goals scored in the head-to-head results. That left a play-off tussle with the Philippines, but no matter, they won 5-0 to take fifth place and qualify for France without conceding a goal.

Winning a third successive Asian Games bronze in August 2018 – with overseas-based high-flyers Cho So-hyun, Ji So-yun and Lee Min-a, plus youth stars Han Chae-rin, Jang Chang and Hong Hye-ji all playing their part – was another boost. If they can all stay fit, Korea Republic will surely build on their successes in 2019.

Above: Ji So-yun, a world-class midfielder and the "national team's treasure".

⊞ NORWAY

Former champions looking to challenge

A nation with a proud pedigree in the international women's game and a full set of silverware to match, their star has faded in recent years. Is it time for Norway to shine once more?

Above: Centre forward Isabell Herlovsen, right, put Norway 2-0 up against the Netherlands in their Group 3 decider.

FEW WOMEN'S teams, besides the USA and Germany, can compete with the achievements of this northern European side: FIFA Women's World Cup™ winners in 1995, European champions in 1987 and 1993 and Sydney 2000 Olympic Games gold medallists.

Although finalists at UEFA Women's EURO 2013, on a global level Norway have performed tamely over the past decade, tumbling out after the group stage in 2011 and then ejected by England in the round of 16 four years later.

Celebrated coach Even Pellerud, whose second reign ended in 2015, achieved success with uncompromisingly direct football. Transforming the team's style in his wake was unlikely to be a

seamless process. His replacement Roger Finjord failed to find favour but Martin Sjögren, appointed in December 2016, has been afforded more time. A dismal early exit at UEFA Women's EURO 2017 – three losses and no goals – plus the blow that 2016 UEFA Best Women's Player Ada Hegerberg no longer wished to represent the national team, were causes for alarm but faith in Sjögren's experience and longer term vision for his talented squad is reaping rewards.

A stoppage-time 1-0 away loss in October 2017, to recently crowned European champions the Netherlands, was the only blemish on their qualifying copybook and an agreement signed in December 2017 granted equal pay to the

THE COACH

MARTIN SJÖGREN
A Swede who has enthusiastically embraced the task of overseeing the generational shift his neighbours are undergoing. Following a playing career in Sweden, as well as a year on a soccer scholarship at the University of North Florida, he switched his skills to coaching in the women's game, starting with Östers IF in 2004. Worked with many top talents during six seasons at LdB FC Malmö (now FC Rosengård) from 2006 and developed a highly-competitive side – which included a healthy crop of Sweden's current, finest young internationals – at Linköpings FC from 2012. He won three league titles and two cups in seven years.

INGRID HJELMSETH
Born: 10 April 1980
Position: Goalkeeper

Excellent custodian, with superb reflexes and a commanding presence. After debuting in 2003, her first major tournament as No.1 was UEFA Women's EURO 2009 in Finland. Such vast experience and her steadfast character make her a crucial member of the squad. Has played her senior club football entirely in Norway – alongside her career as a software engineer – winning league and cup titles with Trondheims-Ørn as well as at current club Stabæk, where she has been for the last decade.

MAREN MJELDE
Born: 6 November 1989
Position: Defender/Midfielder

The team's skipper and most-capped current player. Her composure and versatility is utilised at both centre-back and midfield for club and country – she even made the UEFA Women's EURO 2013 team of the tournament as a full-back – and she delivers pin-point set-pieces. Has played in Norway, Germany and Sweden and was a stand-out performer in Chelsea's FA Women's Super League Spring Series title triumph in 2017 and league and cup double success the following season.

CAROLINE GRAHAM HANSEN
Born: 18 February 1995
Position: Midfielder/Forward

Breakthrough performances established "Caro" as one of the best of her generation at UEFA Women's EURO 2013 but successive injuries limited her playing time in subsequent years, forcing her to miss the FIFA Women's World Cup Canada 2015. A tremendous attacking talent who loves to run at defenders, she picked up silverware at Stabæk (her first aged just 15) and has won multiple league and cup doubles since moving to VfL Wolfsburg in 2014.

WOMEN'S WORLD CUP RECORD		
Year	**Venue**	**Result**
1991	China PR	Runners-up
1995	Sweden	Winners
1999	USA	Fourth place
2003	USA	Quarter-finalists
2007	China PR	Fourth place
2011	Germany	Group stage (3rd, Group D)
2015	Canada	Round of 16

men's and women's squads to round off a bad year on a positive note.

They won every other qualifier before facing the Dutch again in a critical decider the following September. Two goals up within six minutes, they conceded on the half-hour mark and, with the visitors only needing a draw to win the group, battled to hold on for a cathartic victory. "I almost did not stop crying," ecstatic defender Maria Thorisdóttir admitted after the win maintained their status as FIFA Women's World Cup ever-presents.

With unity and belief Norway battled to a better 2018. What could they achieve together in 2019?

Above: Captain Maren Mjelde leads by example.

NIGERIA

Champions of Africa look to roll back the years

Nigeria's battle with Brazil lit up the quarter-finals in 1999 and it was settled by a heartbreaking golden goal. Two decades on, can this generation of *Super Falcons* improve on that best-ever finish?

THE ONLY African side to reach all eight FIFA Women's World Cup™ tournaments, Nigeria are a familiar presence on the global stage. They were made to fight for their place in France, though, as ever-improving rivals South Africa and Cameroon pushed them all the way in qualifying during the Women's Africa Cup of Nations.

Things had changed for the *Super Falcons* since they had last played in – and won – their continental championship under Florence Omagbemi in 2016. They had overcome a pay dispute with the Nigeria Football Federation (NFF) and a fixture-less 2017 and were back in action under new head coach Thomas Dennerby, who was appointed to lead the

side in January 2018 as part of an NFF pledge to boost the women's game and take the national team to another level.

The new man got off to a good start when a home-based group of players delivered bronze at the West African Football Union Women's Cup in February. An 8-0 loss to France with a stronger team two months later was a shock result, but at least a place at the Women's Africa Cup of Nations was secured with an emphatic 7-0 aggregate win over Gambia in June.

When the *Super Falcons* arrived at the tournament proper in mid-November, they had undergone intense training camps and matches against boys' teams. Dennerby's squad included the impressive

Rasheedat Ajibade and three other FIFA U-20 Women's World Cup 2018 quarter-finalists, 13 overseas-based players and the excellent Rivers Angels keeper Tochukwu Oluehi.

THE COACH

THOMAS DENNERBY
A former police officer who has established a reputation as an adaptable, knowledgeable and hard-working football manager. Played for Hammarby IF in the late 1970s until the mid-1980s, gaining UEFA Cup experience along the way. Made his name in the women's game with Djurgården/Älvsjö, leading them to three trophies before taking over as Sweden head coach in 2005. Enjoyed his biggest success with the *Blågult* in 2011 when he led them to FIFA Women's World Cup bronze. Has been tasked with turning the *Super Falcons* into world-beaters and knows what it takes to build winning momentum.

Below: A perennial fixture at the FIFA Women's World Cup, Nigeria know how to turn on the style.

NGOZI OKOBI

Born: 14 December 1993
Position: Midfielder/Forward

The player of the match in the dramatic 3-3 draw with Sweden in Nigeria's opening game at Canada 2015, weighing in with a goal and two assists. Ever present, she won praise after the tournament from FIFA experts for her strength, athleticism and movement. Add versatility and style to that list and it is no wonder she has made a success of spells in Sweden with Vittsjö GIK and Eskilstuna United DFF. She made her debut for Nigeria in 2010 and has played her part in four Women's Africa Cup of Nations title triumphs.

ASISAT OSHOALA

Born: 9 October 1994
Position: Midfielder/Forward

A powerful, speedy attacker with intricate ball skills who can create and score goals from any position. Shone as the Golden Boot and Ball winner at the FIFA U-20 Women's World Cup 2014 and against Sweden at Canada 2015. Has gained valuable overseas experience since then during a Women's FA Cup-winning spell with English side Arsenal, and in China PR with Dalian Quanjian. A three-time African Women's Player of the Year, this football star is an iconic figure for her country.

FRANCISCA ORDEGA

Born: 19 October 1993
Position: Forward

A big-game striker and a clinical finisher, "Franny" was encouraged in her early playing days by her father and is a role model for Nigerians everywhere. Has played in two FIFA Women's World Cups and for club sides across the globe, including Washington Spirit where she has enhanced her reputation with her goals and joyful dance celebrations. Has tested herself further with NWSL off-season loan spells with Atlético Madrid in Spain and Sydney FC in Australia, where she was the W-League's first African player.

Above: Asisat Oshoala will look to shine in a tough FIFA Women's World Cup group.

WOMEN'S WORLD CUP RECORD

Year	Venue	Result
1991	China PR	Group stage (4th, Group C)
1995	Sweden	Group stage (4th, Group B)
1999	USA	Quarter-finalists
2003	USA	Group stage (4th, Group A)
2007	China PR	Group stage (4th, Group B)
2011	Germany	Group stage (3rd, Group A)
2015	Canada	Group stage (4th, Group D)

Theirs was an exciting mix of youth and experience and they duly delivered both qualification for France and another continental crown, but they did so having twice faced the knife-edge of a penalty shoot-out after extra time, first against Cameroon and then against South Africa. Even tougher challenges await Dennerby and his players this summer, but given the right preparation, the *Super Falcons* might just fly high.

GROUP B

Two-time winners Germany are favourites in this group but China PR are their tricky opening opponents and tournament dark horses Spain – the only European side with a 100 per cent record in qualifying – will provide the sternest of tests in Valenciennes on 12 June. First-timers South Africa complete an intriguing quartet.

Main: The Stade Océane was opened in 2012, is the home of Le Havre AC and will have a 25,278 capacity during the FIFA Women's World Cup™.

GERMANY

Is a third world title within their grasp?

Two-time FIFA Women's World Cup™ winners Germany have fallen short in the last two editions of the tournament. Will 2019 be the year this European footballing powerhouse makes it a hat-trick of titles?

THE COACH

MARTINA VOSS-TECKLENBURG
An attack-minded former Germany international who retired on 125 caps with four European titles to her name and experience of playing in three FIFA Women's World Cups. Enjoyed a trophy-laden career as a player and then, as coach of FCR 2001 Duisburg, she won two German Cups and the UEFA Women's Cup. Now 51, she leads Germany having enhanced her reputation during six years as Switzerland head coach. Steered the Swiss to their maiden FIFA Women's World Cup in 2015. Accepted the Germany job in April 2018 but only joined in November after seeing out Switzerland's ultimately unsuccessful bid to reach France 2019.

Above: Die Nationalelf *understand better than most that working together brings success.*

WITH THEIR new coach Martina Voss-Tecklenburg having been in the job for less than seven months, it will be a challenge – but one that the former Switzerland manager and her talented squad are capable of rising to.

The list of players to have hung up their international shirts since Canada 2015 reads like a Who's Who of German football, including as it does Nadine Angerer, Saskia Bartusiak, Melanie Behringer, Nadine Kessler, Annike Krahn, Simone Laudehr, Anja Mittag and Celia Šašić.

Fortunately for Germany, the roll call of those ready to fill their boots is an exciting one, as the qualification campaign for France 2019 proved. Rising stars, who include Linda Dallmann, Kristin Demann, Lina Magull,

Lea Schüller and Carolin Simon, easily complemented a core of established players.

They did not have an easy ride on the road to the finals though, suffering a first qualifying defeat in 19 years when they lost 3-2 to Iceland in October 2017 before a dismal showing at the SheBelieves Cup the following spring led to the dismissal of head coach Steffi Jones.

After so many years of consistency as the managerial succession passed from Gero Bisanz to Tina Theune to Silvia Neid to Jones, Germany were unusually on the rocks. With *Die Nationalelf* having qualified for every edition of the FIFA Women's World Cup, this new generation were under pressure to get back on track.

Horst Hrubesch, who steered the men to Olympic silver in

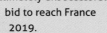

ONES TO WATCH

LINA MAGULL
Born: 15 August 1994
Position: Midfielder

Dortmund-born, goalscoring midfielder who captained Germany to FIFA U-20 Women's World Cup glory in 2014. Having gained top-flight experience during almost three years with VfL Wolfsburg, she won her first senior cap in 2015 and is now regularly called upon thanks to her creativity, style and intelligence. Won praise for her performances at SC Freiburg and in 2018 was snapped up by the club she had supported since childhood, Bayern Munich.

DZSENIFER MAROZSÁN
Born: 18 April 1992
Position: Midfielder

A match winner with intricate ball skills and sublime vision. Scored in the final in Rio as Germany finally won Olympic gold in 2016 having previously played a key role in their UEFA Women's EURO 2013 victory. Missed out on the tail end of qualification for France 2019 having suffered a pulmonary embolism in July 2018, but the two-time German Women's Player of the Year fought her way back to play for club side Olympique Lyonnais three months later.

ALEXANDRA POPP
Born: 6 April 1991
Position: Forward

Worked with Martina Voss-Tecklenburg at FCR 2001 Duisburg a decade ago, winning the UEFA Women's Cup under her stewardship. Has developed into a major player for VfL Wolfsburg and Germany with her powerful aerial threat and versatility. Twice German player of the year, she was sorely missed when a knee injury kept her out of UEFA Women's EURO 2017. Returned looking even fitter and stronger, scoring six goals in qualification for France 2019.

Above: One of the world's most technically gifted midfielders, Dzsenifer Marozsán.

WOMEN'S WORLD CUP RECORD

Year	Venue	Result
1991	China PR	Fourth place
1995	Sweden	Runners-up
1999	USA	Quarter-finalists
2003	USA	Winners
2007	China PR	Winners
2011	Germany	Quarter-finalists
2015	Canada	Fourth place

2016, ensured that they did. As interim coach, the former men's international guided the women to four consecutive qualifying wins to top their group ahead of Iceland, Czech Republic, Slovenia and the Faroe Islands.

As reigning Olympic gold medallists, eight-time European and two-time world champions, Germany are undoubtedly one of the game's great footballing nations. Having shown their bouncebackability in qualifying, where they were the top scorers in Europe, Voss-Tecklenburg's charges look ready to take up the baton. Can they deliver? The world is watching.

CHINA PR

First to qualify and aiming to be last to leave

Once at the vanguard of the international women's game, the *Steel Roses* appear to be on the rise again. Twice hosts, and finalists in 1999, they are sure to be tricky opponents for any side in France.

Above: *High fives for China's hotshot No.10 Li Ying.*

THE FIRST EVER FIFA Women's World Cup™ was held in China in 1991, and the Chinese also featured in the famous 1999 final against the USA – a game that inspired many of the current generation of *Steel Roses*, who were schoolgirls at the time.

China's failure to qualify for the 2011 tournament marked a nadir in their attempts to restore the national side back amongst the elite but the resilient young squad that made the quarter-finals four years ago, going out 1-0 to eventual champions USA, suggested that brighter prospects lay ahead.

Standards and investment in the domestic league have also risen since the Chinese Women's Super League was relaunched in 2015, and that promising group

of players have continued to evolve – typified by captain and right back/central defender Wu Haiyan's maturing leadership and the potency of the team's many exciting attacking talents.

China PR were the first team to qualify – besides hosts France – for the 2019 tournament by topping their group at the AFC Women's Asian Cup in April 2018 with wins over Thailand and the Philippines. The disappointment of losing 3-1 in the semi-finals to regional rivals Japan was tempered by beating Thailand again in the play-off for third place.

Icelandic coach Sigurður Ragnar Eyjólfsson, who had been in charge from November 2017 departed shortly after and was replaced by Jia Xiuquan.

THE COACH

JIA XIUQUAN

Former defender who gained 55 caps, captained his country and was named most valuable player at the 1984 AFC Asian Cup. Broke ground by being one of the first Chinese footballers to play in Europe (for Yugoslavia's Partizan in 1988) and the first in Japan's J.League (for Gamba Osaka) in the early 1990s. Respected for his overseas experience he has coached many of the Chinese national youth sides as well as Henan Jianye and Shanghai Shenhua in the men's Super League. His appointment in May 2018 raised eyebrows as the *Steel Roses* marked his first foray into the women's game.

ONES TO WATCH

WANG SHUANG
Born: 23 January 1995
Position: Midfielder

A graceful playmaker and neat finisher with fantastic vision and excellent free kicks. Joined Paris Saint-Germain in August 2018 from her hometown side Wuhan Jiangda. Has played for Sportstoto in the Korean WK League and was part of Dalian Quanjian's 2016 and 2017 CWSL title-winning teams. Her goal in a 1-0 win in 2015 ended the USA's 104-match unbeaten streak on home soil, in Abby Wambach's farewell game. Named 2018 AFC Women's Player of the Year.

WANG SHANSHAN
Born: 27 January 1990
Position: Midfielder/Forward

Started out as a defender but was used as a speedy No.9 for the team at Canada 2015. Now more often deployed on the right of the frontline or in midfield. Won gold at the 2011 Summer Universiade (World University Games) in China before making her senior team debut the following year. Strong, tenacious and brave in the air, she netted an incredible nine times after coming on as a second-half substitute against Tajikistan on the way to being top scorer with 12 goals in six games at the 2018 Asian Games.

LI YING
Born: 7 January 1993
Position: Forward

Scored seven, at least one in each of China's five games (including two penalties), to finish as the leading scorer at the AFC Women's Asian Cup 2018, a remarkable tally that firmly established her as the *Steel Roses'* go-to target player up front. From Chongqing, the live-wire centre forward, like Wang Shuang, spent a season playing professionally in the Korea Republic (with Suwon in 2014) but returned in 2015 and now plays for Shandong Sports Lottery in her homeland.

WOMEN'S WORLD CUP RECORD

Year	Venue	Result
1991	China PR	Quarter-finalists
1995	Sweden	Fourth place
1999	USA	Runners-up
2003	USA	Quarter-finalists
2007	China PR	Quarter-finalists
2011	Germany	Did not qualify
2015	Canada	Quarter-finalists

His emphasis on teamwork and enthusiasm to develop tactics to make them competitive against the best was tested immediately with two June friendlies in the USA (they lost both by one-goal margins) and then August's 2018 Asian Games in Indonesia. It took a 90th-minute goal for Japan to grab the 1-0 win in a tense final. Jia's team were in tears but they won silver, their best finish for 16 years.

Who knows, maybe the world's most populous nation is gearing up to make a surprise impact at women's football's biggest showcase...

Above: A true talent and joy to watch: playmaker Wang Shuang.

SPAIN

Could Spain be ready to spring a surprise?

Spain did not get beyond the group stage on their FIFA Women's World Cup™ bow in 2015 but much has changed in the years since, and *La Roja* are now considered one of Europe's hottest properties.

THE COACH

JORGE VILDA
Nominated for the FIFA Women's World Coach of the Year award on three occasions, the 37-year-old has worked his magic on Spain since taking the reins in 2015. A knee condition put paid to his dreams of becoming a professional footballer but he took to coaching with ease and is described as a born winner, meticulous planner and smart strategist. Enjoyed immense success with Spain's youth sides, winning three European titles as well as bronze and silver at the FIFA U-17 Women's World Cup in 2010 and 2014 respectively. He will have prepared his team with care.

Above: Spain qualified for France 2019 with a 100 per cent record.

THE ONLY EUROPEAN nation to finish their France 2019 qualifying campaign with a victory in every match, this vibrant and exciting national side were also the first to book their ticket to this summer's tournament.

"Yes, yes, yes, we cannot be happier," tweeted Spain's official account in June 2018 once *La Roja*'s second consecutive FIFA Women's World Cup finals appearance was confirmed with two games in hand. A 2-0 win over Israel coupled with Austria's victory over Finland settled it and with nearly 8,000 interactions, there was a definite thumbs-up for the celebratory message on social media.

In the course of topping a group featuring Austria, Finland, Serbia and Israel, Spain had delivered a whopping 25 goals for with just two against. It was not entirely surprising, because with their high-tempo, counter-attacking and intense defensive style, *La Roja* have been buoyant under head coach Jorge Vilda.

Installed in 2015 after their disappointing FIFA Women's World Cup debut, Vilda has managed to blend experienced players such as Marta Corredera and Irene Paredes with former youth starlets like midfielder "Patri" Guijarro and striker Olga García, and the results have been impressive.

In 2017, Spain won the Algarve Cup and reached the quarter-finals of the UEFA Women's EURO, going out after a penalty shoot-out with Austria. It was a cruel blow, but

ONES TO WATCH

PATRICIA GUIJARRO
Born: 17 May 1998
Position: Midfielder

An energetic box-to-box midfielder capable of turning a match with a drop of her shoulder. Only 21 but an ever-present in qualifying and has gained big game experience during her time at club side FC Barcelona and with Spain's youth teams. Silver medallist at both the FIFA U-17 Women's World Cup 2014 and the U-20 edition four years later where she won the adidas Golden Boot and Ball awards. Also scored two, one the winner, against France to seal UEFA Women's Under-19 Championship gold in 2017.

AMANDA SAMPEDRO
Born: 26 June 1993
Position: Midfielder

A joyful player capable of wreaking havoc by switching flanks or driving through the middle. Captained Spain to UEFA European Women's Under-17 Championship glory under Jorge Vilda in 2010, lifting the trophy on her 17th birthday. Part of Spain's squad for the last three major tournaments, she is now a key performer, playing all but one minute of their EURO 2017 campaign. Debuted for Atlético Madrid aged 15, she has gone on to skipper her hometown club to league and cup titles.

JENNIFER HERMOSO
Born: 9 May 1990
Position: Midfielder/Forward

The team DJ is a highly respected left-footed attacker who provided nine assists in qualifying and scored seven times. Has hit some crucial goals at club level too, including the one that won the title for Rayo Vallecano in 2011. A two-time champion with FC Barcelona, she was also the league's top scorer two seasons running. Tested herself in the Swedish league with Tyresö FF and at Paris Saint-Germain in France before returning to Spanish champions Atlético Madrid.

WOMEN'S WORLD CUP RECORD

Year	Venue	Result
1991	China PR	Did not qualify
1995	Sweden	Did not qualify
1999	USA	Did not qualify
2003	USA	Did not qualify
2007	China PR	Did not qualify
2011	Germany	Did not qualify
2015	Canada	Group stage (4th, Group E)

Vilda's charges bounced back, pipping Italy to the 12-nation 2018 Cyprus Cup title in the midst of coolly delivering qualification for this summer's world showpiece in France.

Of course, with success comes expectation and hopes are high in Spain where the U-19s and U-17s were both European champions in 2018 and football is the fastest growing sport for females. The top flight is thriving too with gains in professionalism, reputation and media attention following backing by *La Liga* and Iberdrola and investment from men's clubs. If the national side can progress on the world stage, further gains will surely follow.

Above: Patricia "Patri" Guijarro is one of the exciting young talents emerging from Spain.

SOUTH AFRICA

Banyana Banyana carry the best wishes of a proud nation

Like *Bafana Bafana* 21 years ago, South Africa's women have qualified for their first senior World Cup, also in France. After years of striving to be there, they will want to make every kick count.

NAMED 2018 South African Sports Awards Team of the Year, *Banyana Banyana* have achieved considerable regional success in their history, claiming the COSAFA Women's Championship for Southern African nations five times. They have also finished as runners-up in continental competitions, but FIFA Women's World Cup™ qualification has always been the ultimate aim.

Narrowly missing Canada 2015 after losing 1-0 to a late goal against Côte d'Ivoire was a bitter blow, though that disappointment further fuelled the hunger this time around. Outings at the last two Olympics, sustained backing from the South African Football Association and their sponsors and sound preparation by coach Desiree Ellis and her squad ensured that *Banyana Banyana* were ready.

Confirmed as full-time successor to Dutch coach Vera Pauw in February 2018 after 16 months as interim manager, Ellis embraced the pressure of the year ahead, stating that qualification for France 2019 was "non-negotiable".

They booked their place at the Women's Africa Cup of Nations Ghana 2018 by dismissing Lesotho 7-0 on aggregate in qualifying and then defended their COSAFA crown on home soil in September, beating guest participants Cameroon 2-1 in the final. When November arrived, it was crunch time in Ghana and with only three spots available for France 2019, *Banyana Banyana* needed a good start in a tough group.

A 1-0 win in only their second ever victory over Nigeria

THE COACH

DESIREE ELLIS

A former national team player and captain who made her international debut aged 30 in 1993, scoring a hat-trick in a 14-0 win over Swaziland in *Banyana Banyana's* first-ever match. She earned 32 caps and retired in 2002 but her dedication and infectious passion for football meant this was only the first chapter. Having played for her last club, Cape Town-based Spurs, for over a decade, she then managed them for a similar period before joining the national team as assistant in 2014. The only South African to win COSAFA Cups as a player and coach, in 2002 and then in 2017 and 2018.

Below: Banyana Banyana *have finally qualified for their first FIFA Women's World Cup.*

ONES TO WATCH

JANINE VAN WYK
Born: 17 April 1987
Position: Defender

South Africa's most-capped player with over 150 appearances for her country. A fearless centre-back and good reader of the game, she has captained the team since 2013. Joined her first senior team, Springs Home Sweepers in the township of KwaThema, aged just 14 and was the only white girl in the league. Founded a development programme for girls in Gauteng province in 2012 and a SAFA Sasol Women's League club in 2013, the eponymously named JVW FC. Spent 2017 and 2018 with Houston Dash in the USA.

REFILOE JANE
Born: 4 August 1992
Position: Midfielder

Soweto-born, petite and technical midfielder who was first scouted and selected for the national team ahead of the London 2012 Olympics and has since become an integral part of the side. Wore the armband in the 2017 COSAFA Women's Championship success and scored twice in the final in 2018. "Fifi" as she is known, is studying for a masters in sports management and marketing at Tshwane University of Technology. Completed a "dream move" to Canberra United in the W-League in the summer of 2018.

THEMBI KGATLANA
Born: 2 May 1996
Position: Forward

Rapid, exciting and raw young striker who signed for Houston Dash in the American NWSL in February 2018 and, along with highly regarded playmaker Linda Motlhalo, was offered a contract extension for 2019. She is capable of outrageous skill, like her match-winner in their opener against Nigeria at the Women's Africa Cup of Nations 2018. Hit a crucial strike against Mali and finished as the event's top scorer with five goals, picking up player of the tournament too. Named African Women's Player of the Year 2018.

guaranteed they got that. It was a committed, structured performance and established a benchmark for the tournament and beyond.

Brushing aside Equatorial Guinea 7-1 and drawing 1-1 with Zambia meant a showdown with Mali in the semi-final. The Malians were no match for Ellis' side though, and a 2-0 win secured the all-important ticket to France 2019.

Nigeria lifted the trophy after a shoot-out in the final but the upwardly mobile *Banyana Banyana* had achieved their goal and were treated to a heroines' welcome when they landed back in Johannesburg. The nation will be behind them once again in June.

Left: South Africa's thrilling and gifted young forward, Thembi Kgatlana.

WOMEN'S WORLD CUP RECORD
Though they came within one game of the finals last time out, this is the first time that South Africa have qualified for the FIFA Women's World Cup.

GROUP C

Top seeds Australia are carrying high expectations and begin their campaign against a rejuvenated Italy team returning to the world stage after a 20-year absence. Meanwhile, the rhythm of the *Reggae Girlz* will meet the samba beat on 9 June in Grenoble when South American champions Brazil play debutants Jamaica.

Main: Grenoble's Stade des Alpes is situated in the city centre and boasts a stunning mountainous backdrop.

AUSTRALIA

Time to deliver for promising generation

Australia have been considered plucky underdogs in the past but after three consecutive quarter-final appearances at the FIFA Women's World Cup™ and recent wins against the world's best, will the *Matildas* be waltzing towards silverware in France?

AUSTRALIA ENSURED they would be heading to their seventh FIFA Women's World Cup with a 1-1 draw, courtesy of Sam Kerr's late leveller, in a group-stage tussle with fellow qualifiers Japan, at the AFC Women's Asian Cup in April 2018.

Confederation bragging rights were up for grabs as they faced the *Nadeshiko* again in the final. Despite dominating, they lost 1-0, a repeat of their elimination from Canada 2015.

They achieved the main objective of 2018, albeit without regaining the trophy they had won in 2010, but 2017 was the year when it felt as if Australia had really "arrived". Unbeaten throughout a stellar 12 months, their triumph at the invitational 2017 Tournament of Nations was the highlight. They outplayed the USA and won 1-0 – their first-ever conquest over the hosts in almost 30 years – then thumped Japan 4-2 and Brazil 6-1. Regardless of its "friendly" status, this competition success elevated expectations of the *Matildas* from within and without and lifted them to fourth in the world ranking, their highest-ever placing.

The USA edged them on goals scored when Australia attempted to defend the title the following year. Meanwhile, head coach Alen Stajcic carried on developing his squad, testing new combinations and integrating youthful talent alongside maturing quality. For example, Australia's all-time top scorer Lisa De Vanna, looking to figure in her fourth finals, has shared the field with schoolgirls Mary Fowler and Amy Sayer.

THE COACH

ALEN STAJCIC
A former schoolboy international, "Staj" played in the New South Wales Premier League before embarking on a flourishing coaching journey which progressed via the NSW Institute of Sport women's football programme, the NSW Sapphires, the *Young Matildas* and then Sydney FC, from the W-League's inaugural season in 2008 onwards. Six years and two championships later, he was brought in as interim coach for the senior side a month before the AFC Women's Asian Cup 2014. He impressed and was taken on full-time from that September. Former *Socceroo* Gary Van Egmond and father of *Matildas* midfielder Emily is his assistant.

Below: Striker Sam Kerr has been in "flipping" fantastic form.

ONES TO WATCH

LYDIA WILLIAMS
Born: 13 May 1988
Position: Goalkeeper

With an American mother and a native Australian father, she bears a tattoo on her left wrist of her Aboriginal middle name Yilkari (meaning "heaven" or "sky"). Grew up in Western Australia then Canberra, so Canberra United was her W-League team in between seasons in America's National Women's Soccer League, although in 2016 she switched to Melbourne City FC. Signed for Seattle Reign FC in 2017 and was named in the NWSL Second XI in 2018. She is the brave base upon which the *Matildas* are built.

ELISE KELLOND-KNIGHT
Born: 10 August 1990
Position: Defender/Midfielder

Debuted aged 16 in 2007 and has consistently impressed since, making the FIFA Women's World Cup All-Star squad in both 2011 and 2015. Earned her 100th cap in October 2018. A well-respected leader and versatile too – comfortable as a holding midfielder or left back – her club career has included W-League championships with Brisbane Roar FC in 2009 and 2011, plus time in Denmark, Germany, Japan and Sweden. Signed for Melbourne City FC and then Seattle Reign FC in 2018-19.

SAM KERR
Born: 10 September 1993
Position: Forward

First-rate finisher with searing pace and fine heading ability. "Without question the world's most dangerous player in the front third," says Stajcic. Actually started out playing Australian rules football (her father and brother were professionals) but switched to "soccer" aged 12 and appeared for the *Matildas* at 15. The NWSL's all-time leading scorer, awarded the 2017 AFC Women's Player of the Year award amongst many other recent accolades, including 2018 Young Australian of the Year.

A collective bargaining agreement reached in September 2017 has improved conditions and competitiveness in the W-League, while many established internationals alternate biannually between domestic action in Australia and the USA's NWSL.

Renowned for their high-intensity, athletic style, Australia are no longer the hungry rookies with future intentions. Could we see backflips from striker Sam Kerr celebrating more than just goals in France?

WOMEN'S WORLD CUP RECORD

Year	Venue	Result
1991	China PR	Did not qualify
1995	Sweden	Group stage (4th, Group C)
1999	USA	Group stage (3rd, Group D)
2003	USA	Group stage (4th, Group D)
2007	China PR	Quarter-finalists
2011	Germany	Quarter-finalists
2015	Canada	Quarter-finalists

Above: Lydia Williams is a solid presence between the sticks for the Matildas.

ITALY

Ambitious Italians aiming high

Italy were quarter-finalists in 1991 but last stepped out at a FIFA Women's World Cup™ two decades ago. After sailing through qualification, how far can *Le Azzurre* go in their third finals appearance?

Above: Sheer joy as Italy qualify for France 2019.

HEAD COACH Milena Bertolini has targeted the knockout stage in France and, if all goes well, the former defender hopes to make Italy a footballing force to be reckoned with in the years to come. A veteran of the top flight *Serie A* in the 1990s, Bertolini no doubt remembers her national side's heyday when, following their FIFA Women's World Cup 1991 quarter-final adventure in China, they were runners-up at the 1993 and 1997 UEFA European Women's Championships.

Although ever present at all subsequent EUROs, Italy have been absent from the world stage since 1999. *Le Azzurre*'s renaissance has been coming though, and after losing in play-offs for the 2011 and 2015 editions of this competition,

they were the second European team to qualify after a truly emphatic qualification campaign.

So defensively strong, clinical and united were Italy that they went into their penultimate match against Portugal in Florence in June 2018 unbeaten, knowing that a win would see them through. Players who had competed in Italy's first women's championship and played for the national team back in 1968 were among the 6,500-strong crowd at the Stadio Artemio Franchi that night and when Barbara Bonansea scored in stoppage time to make it 3-0, Italy's destiny was assured. Cue celebratory knee slides across the pitch and fist pumping salutes to the stands from the players, who tossed Bertolini

THE COACH

MILENA BERTOLINI
Former central defender with decades of experience as a player and coach in the Italian top flight. Won a raft of titles playing for a host of teams in *Serie A* and has won silverware at every turn since kicking off her coaching career with Foroni Verona in 2001. Crowned "Golden Bench" coach of the year six times by the Italian FA. Left Brescia after a successful five-year spell to succeed FIFA World Cup winner Antonio Cabrini as Italy head coach in August 2017 and has made a seamless transition from club football to the national team.

ONES TO WATCH

SARA GAMA
Born: 27 March 1989
Position: Defender

Captain of Italy and Juventus, this foreign languages and literature graduate boasts bags of big game experience and has won *Serie A* with both Brescia and Juve. Captained Italy to victory in the UEFA Women's Under-19 Championship in 2008 and was named player of the tournament. Has experience of three UEFA Women's EUROs, and has played for Paris Saint-Germain and Juve in the UEFA Women's Champions League. A Barbie doll was made in her image for International Women's Day.

ALICE PARISI
Born: 11 December 1990
Position: Midfielder

Technical, visionary and free-scoring midfielder who will be raring to go after nearly a year out with a broken leg suffered against England in 2017. Scored the winner in Italy's historic UEFA Women's Under-19 Championship victory in 2008. Has also won silverware with club sides Bardolino Verona, Tavagnacco and Fiorentina. Crowned the "Golden Girl" Italian player of 2013, nominated for the 2016 *Pallone Azzuro* best Italy player award and the 2017 FIFPro Women's World XI.

BARBARA BONANSEA
Born: 13 June 1991
Position: Forward

A nippy and energetic footballer who displayed her remarkable repertoire of tricks, great first touch and eye for goal in qualifying. Gained UEFA Women's Champions League experience under Milena Bertolini at Brescia and made history as the first Juventus player to score in the competition in September 2018, with not one but two goals against Brøndby IF. Shone for Italy in a tough group at EURO 2017 and was top scorer for Juve in her debut season in 2017-18 as they were crowned *Serie A* champions.

Above: Fleet of foot, Barbara Bonansea will test the best.

WOMEN'S WORLD CUP RECORD

Year	Venue	Result
1991	China PR	Quarter-finalists
1995	Sweden	Did not qualify
1999	USA	Group stage (3rd Group B)
2003	USA	Did not qualify
2007	China PR	Did not qualify
2011	Germany	Did not qualify
2015	Canada	Did not qualify

high into the air like a rag doll in celebration.

Speaking in Rome soon after, Bertolini was already looking ahead to France as she unveiled plans to invite the country's 46 best young players to a training camp. With so many getting the chance to develop in a resurgent league set-up spurred on by the Italian FA and involvement of men's clubs Fiorentina, Juventus, AC Milan and AS Roma (where legendary USA striker Mia Hamm is a board member), Italy could well become a global player in women's football again. What better time to kick-start a revival than this summer?

BRAZIL

Bringing their flair and samba style to France

Never short on natural talent, Brazil have often thrilled and entertained at the FIFA Women's World Cup™ but have yet to achieve top billing. Could 2019 be the year *As Canarinhas* live up to expectations?

THE COACH

OSWALDO ALVAREZ

First in charge from 2014 until after Rio 2016, this is his second stint as coach of the *Seleção* and will be his second FIFA Women's World Cup with the team. In his first 12 games back in charge after replacing Emily Lima in September 2017, the team won 11 matches, drew one and claimed two titles. Known as "Vadão" the 62-year-old has worked in Brazilian football across three decades, including spells at men's clubs such as Corinthians, São Paulo and Atlético Paranaense. He is viewed as an adaptable coach, great at problem-solving and encouraging of youthful talent, having brought through famous names like Kaká and Rivaldo.

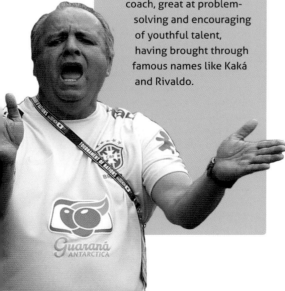

Above: As Canarinhas *celebrate their* Copa América Femenina 2018 *success.*

CLINCHING THEIR seventh *Copa América Femenina* in April 2018 ensured Brazil maintained their ever-present record at the FIFA Women's World Cup, guaranteeing a spot at the Tokyo 2020 Olympic Games in the process, but they are yet to win a global gold.

For years, many lamented the lack of backing for Brazil's skilful women from the Brazilian FA (CBF). The creation of a permanent selection programme before Canada 2015 and the home Olympics in August 2016 suggested a sea change and over 70,000 fans were at the Maracana to cheer Marta and Co. on in the Rio semi-finals (they lost to Sweden in a shoot-out), showing some of the potential of the team and also the women's game, both on the field and off.

Emily Lima, the first woman to coach *As Canarinhas*, was appointed post Rio but sacked less than a year later due to poor results. Oswaldo Alvarez was reinstated as coach, got his players onside and has set to work on developing their tactical versatility – the majority of his squad now play professionally overseas so their conditioning is no longer a pressing priority. His first success after returning was overseeing two wins and a draw in October 2017, which gave them victory in China's Yongchuan International Tournament.

Brazil's seven wins, 31 goals for and just two against reflects the ease with which they triumphed at the *Copa América Femenina* in Chile. Fourteen players contributed to that scoring tally, underlining the team's dynamic positive play.

ONES TO WATCH

ANDRESSINHA
Born: 1 May 1995
Position: Midfielder

Grew up in the southern Brazil state of Rio Grande do Sul and, like Marta, started in futsal playing against boys and her masterful ball control reflects that. Great at set pieces and striking from distance. Credits her father Elizeu Machry for believing in her talent when younger and making vast round trips to take her to training and games. Captained Brazil at a number of FIFA Women's World Cups at youth level, played in all four games at Canada 2015 and joined Houston Dash shortly after. Moved to Portland Thorns in January 2018.

BEATRIZ
Born: 17 December 1993
Position: Forward

"Bia" is a physical forward who leads Brazil's front line. Made only one and two substitute appearances respectively at the FIFA Women's World Cups in 2011 and 2015 but by Rio 2016 had secured a regular starting spot, scoring three times – including in the bronze medal match loss to Canada. The goals have continued to flow, her six in qualifying only bettered by Catalina Usme of Colombia. A championship winner in the Korean WK League with Incheon Hyundai Steel for six successive seasons, starting from 2013.

MARTA
Born: 19 February 1986
Position: Forward

Six-time FIFA Women's World Player of the Year/The Best FIFA Women's Player and has won numerous individual awards and championships in Sweden, where she gained citizenship in March 2017, and in the USA. Ominously for opponents, she is in some of the best form of her career at Orlando Pride in America's NWSL. Ferociously skilful and fast on the ball, her left foot can be a precision weapon. Already sitting pretty as all-time competition top scorer with 15 goals in four finals.

Above: Brazil's No.10, Marta, the greatest player the women's game has ever seen?

WOMEN'S WORLD CUP RECORD

Year	Venue	Result
1991	China PR	Group stage (3rd, Group B)
1995	Sweden	Group stage (4th, Group A)
1999	USA	Third place
2003	USA	Quarter-finalists
2007	China PR	Runners-up
2011	Germany	Quarter-finalists
2015	Canada	Round of 16

Results from further afield in friendlies against higher-ranked opponents have been topsy-turvy but they are getting games in, learning and growing in strength.

For some, this could be their last major tournament. Iconic forwards Marta and Cristiane, defenders Mônica, Tamires and Érika, and goalkeeper Bárbara are all aged 30 or over and Paris Saint-Germain's seemingly indefatigable defensive midfielder Formiga will be 41 and could make history if selected for a record seventh FIFA Women's World Cup. Can they write the perfect ending in 2019?

⚔ JAMAICA

Reggae Girlz ready to make their own bit of history

In 1998, Jamaica's men played in their first FIFA World Cup™. Now, the women's team have performed another of the nation's greatest sporting feats, defying the odds and following in the footsteps of the *Reggae Boyz* to the same destination.

THE COACH

HUE MENZIES

A Jamaican coach with experience in the USA stretching over three decades. Played at Hardin-Simmons University in Texas, coaching while in college to earn extra cash. Spent six years working in banking, before quitting the corporate world to return to his passion and full-time coaching. Has helped hundreds of young players enter the college game in the USA during his career. Executive director of Florida Kraze Krush soccer club and also coach of the Florida Krush senior women's team, he was initially asked to join the Jamaican women's programme as technical director by Cedella Marley, after the team failed to qualify for Canada 2015.

"THIS IS WAY MORE THAN FOOTBALL," declared a jubilant Hue Menzies, head coach of the history-making *Reggae Girlz*, the first-ever Caribbean team to qualify for the FIFA Women's World Cup™. While his players sang and danced in celebration, social media was flooded with messages of congratulations, including felicitations from the world's fastest man, Usain Bolt.

The team had been disbanded in 2010 due to lack of funds and was inactive until Cedella Marley, the daughter of legendary singer Bob Marley, offered her support and financial backing and resurrected the programme in 2014. They fell short in Canada 2015 qualifying but with an injection of young and overseas-based talent into the squad, they embarked on the road to France in May 2018 with renewed impetus. In one game in the Caribbean Zone first round, they found themselves 2-0 down to home side Haiti. Instead of crumbling they battled back to draw 2-2. This was a turning point in their campaign and they then hosted and coasted through the final Caribbean stage.

Jamaica were ranked sixth in the North American confederation and only three automatic places at France 2019 were on offer at the Concacaf Women's Championship in the USA in October. In group play, they lost 2-0 to Canada, surprised many by beating much-fancied Costa Rica 1-0 and dismissed Cuba 9-0. Their semi-final

Below: Team-mates mob Dominique Bond-Flasza, who netted the decisive penalty to book Jamaica's ticket to their first FIFA Women's World Cup.

ONES TO WATCH

KONYA PLUMMER
Born: 2 August 1997
Position: Defender

The *Reggae Girlz* centre-back, skipper and defensive anchor is also dangerous when coming forward at set pieces. Goes by the nickname "Country" due to her rural roots. A natural leader, her first taste of organised football was aged 11 with a boys' team, and within two years she was their captain. She attends the University of Central Florida, also playing for Menzies' Florida Krush. One of four Jamaicans who started all five of their 2018 Concacaf Women's Championship games, she made more interceptions than any other player.

KHADIJA SHAW
Born: 31 January 1997
Position: Midfielder/Forward

Known as "Bunny" because of her love of carrots, at 5' 11" she is an imposing striker. Featured for Jamaica's U-15s, U-17s and U-20s all while aged 14. Moved to the USA to play junior college soccer before starting a scholarship at the University of Tennessee in 2017. Included in the All-SEC (Southeastern Conference) First Team in her first season and named 2018 SEC offensive player of the year. Top scorer in all France 2019 qualifying with 19 goals in the Caribbean Zone and Concacaf Women's Championship combined.

JODY BROWN
Born: 16 April 2002
Position: Forward

The nimble young forward hinted at her potential in 2014 when, aged 12, she became the first player to bag four goals in a single match at the Concacaf Girls' U-15 Championship. With four goals she was Jamaica's top markswoman at the 2018 Concacaf Women's Championship where she won the young player of the tournament award. Started a scholarship at Montverde Academy near Orlando, USA, in August 2017 and will be just 17 in France. Made one goal and scored the other in the historic win over Panama.

defeat to the hosts was a 6-0 one-sided affair but there was still the third-place match against Panama to come, with a ticket to France to play for.

Khadija Shaw's header and Jody Brown's strike put them ahead twice but the game ended 2-2. With minutes remaining and a shoot-out looming, Menzies boldly switched goalkeepers, bringing on Nicole McClure for teenager Sydney Schneider, who had been superb against Costa Rica. The substitute "saved" the day, stopping two of Panama's spot kicks before defender Dominique Bond-Flasza buried the decisive penalty.

Theirs is an inspiring story of triumph over adversity. What does the next chapter hold for the *Reggae Girlz*?

WOMEN'S WORLD CUP RECORD
Jamaica have finally qualified for their first-ever FIFA Women's World Cup at their sixth attempt. They did not enter in 1999 or 2011.

Above: Determined and deserving of her place on the world stage, Khadija Shaw was the highest scorer in qualifying for France 2019.

GROUP D

—————— //// ——————

Rivalries abound in this group so expect fireworks in Nice on 9 June when debutants Scotland face "auld enemy" England, and again ten days later when the *Lionesses* go toe-to-toe with their Canada 2015 semi-final vanquishers Japan. Keep an eye on Argentina and Scotland, though, as both are chasing a first win on the world stage.

Main: The Stade de Nice hosted several matches during UEFA EURO 2016. Now this modern arena, also home to OGC Nice, welcomes the FIFA Women's World Cup™.

 ENGLAND

Lionesses look to roar their way to the top

At Canada 2015 the *Lionesses* suffered a heartbreaking semi-final loss to Japan through a freakish own goal but bounced back to beat Germany to take bronze. Having reached the semi-finals of UEFA Women's EURO 2017, they believe they can go even further in France.

ENGLAND WERE AGAIN unbeaten during their FIFA Women's World Cup™ qualifying campaign, and have now not lost a qualifier since slipping to a 1-0 away defeat to France in the play-off final for the FIFA Women's World Cup 2003. In qualifying for France 2019, they racked up 29 goals and conceded just one – only Germany scored more in the UEFA qualifying round and no team's defence was as stingy.

Those statistics suggest a seamless road to France but things got off to a bumpy start, with head coach Mark Sampson controversially dismissed – for matters unrelated to performance – just hours after their opening 6-0 win over Russia in September 2017. *Lionesses* youth coach Mo Marley oversaw routine wins over Bosnia and Herzegovina and Kazakhstan before former men's professional Phil Neville was offered the role.

Neville's involvement captured the interest of the wider football media, as did an unexpected Group 1 leadership challenge from next-door neighbours Wales who held England 0-0 in Southampton and were also undefeated until the *Lionesses*' 3-0 win in the reverse fixture confirmed their supremacy and top spot.

Neville has offered opportunities to previously untried and developing talent: 34 players saw action in qualifying, including seven players who made their debuts in the 6-0 win in Kazakhstan. Players like skipper Steph Houghton, Jill Scott and EURO 2017 Golden Boot winner Jodie Taylor offer a spine of maturity and

THE COACH

PHIL NEVILLE

Former England, Manchester United and Everton full-back/midfielder who spent a trophy-laden decade of his 19-year career under legendary manager Sir Alex Ferguson. Sparked something of a furore when appointed head coach in January 2018 – his previous experience in the dugout limited to assistant roles in the men's game – but the *Lionesses* took to him immediately. Went to three UEFA European Championships as a player but this will be his first World Cup. Younger brother to fellow former England defender Gary and twin to Tracey, an ex-player and coach of the successful England netball team.

Below: The Lionesses *squad has matured together since Canada 2015.*

ONES TO WATCH

LUCY BRONZE
Born: 28 October 1991
Position: Defender

Athletic, attack-minded right back whose ultra-competitive attitude is belied by her laid-back, off-the-field nature. Lives up to her middle name (her mother's maiden name) of Tough. Born in Northumberland to an English mother and a Portuguese father she enjoyed European and domestic success in her first season at Olympique Lyonnais in 2017-18. Started at Sunderland and won championships with Liverpool and Manchester City, where she established herself as a world-class talent.

FRAN KIRBY
Born: 29 June 1993
Position: Forward

Chelsea's talented, technically skilled and prolific striker. Graduated through the youth sides at Reading. Dubbed England's "mini Messi" after her goal against Mexico at Canada 2015. Bubbly character who has bravely spoken out about depression and coping with the sudden death of her mother. Hit superlative form in 2017-18, scoring 25 in all competitions, collecting a number of national player of the year awards and cementing her place as a true fans' favourite.

NIKITA PARRIS
Born: 10 March 1994
Position: Forward

A striker from Liverpool who is now a very effective right-sided forward. Passionate, pacy, deceptively dangerous in the air and with a poacher's instinct, "Keets" joined Everton at 14, making her first-team debut in August 2010. Joined Manchester City on loan in January 2015 and signed permanently a year later. She led the *Lionesses* with six goals in qualifying and edged ahead of Eniola Aluko to become the FA WSL's all-time top scorer in November 2018. Her older sister is Olympic boxer Natasha Jonas.

experience, while Nikita Parris (their top scorer with six in qualifying), Millie Bright and Keira Walsh are emerging stars.

A reboot of the elite leagues in England saw a fully professional FA Women's Super League established for the 2018-19 season, the country will host the UEFA Women's EURO 2021, a number of *Lionesses* are excelling in club football overseas and England won bronze at the FIFA U-20 Women's World Cup 2018.

England have momentum and expect to be in the mix in France but as their boss has clearly stated: "Third will not be good enough".

Left: Lucy Bronze, England's right back but influential all over the park.

WOMEN'S WORLD CUP RECORD

Year	Venue	Result
1991	China PR	Did not qualify
1995	Sweden	Quarter-finalists
1999	USA	Did not qualify
2003	USA	Did not qualify
2007	China PR	Quarter-finalists
2011	Germany	Quarter-finalists
2015	Canada	Third place

SCOTLAND

Flying the flag for an excited nation

Scotland have made history by qualifying for their first FIFA Women's World Cup™. A never-say-die attitude carried them through a tough campaign, but can they put in another "braveheart" performance on their finals bow?

THE COACH

SHELLEY KERR

This UEFA Pro Licence holder had already played alongside or coached most of the squad before replacing Anna Signeul, who announced before EURO 2017 that she would step down after the tournament. A respected former centre-back, 49-year-old Kerr won every domestic Scottish honour and represented her country 59 times. Gained international experience coaching Scotland's Under-19s. Former head coach of Arsenal, where she won two FA Women's Cups and a League Cup, and of Stirling University, becoming the first woman in Britain to manage a men's league team. Loves to work outside her comfort zone and will relish every minute of France 2019.

Above: History in the making for Shelley Kerr and Scotland.

HAVING COME within touching distance of the FIFA Women's World Cup 2015 and two UEFA Women's EUROs only to lose in the play-offs, Scotland will definitely be driven to prove themselves this summer. They arrive in France with experience of one major tournament under their belt, EURO 2017. Then, an understrength squad lost heavily to England, but returned home pondering what might have been after a narrow loss to Portugal and an impressive win over Spain.

Now, they are ready to go again, this time with former Scotland captain Shelley Kerr at the helm and off the back of a qualification campaign that saw defensive rocks Jen Beattie and Emma Mitchell, talismanic midfielder

Kim Little and winger Lizzie Arnot return from injury to bolster a squad blessed with youth and experience.

It had been a rollercoaster of a qualification ride, from losing 1-0 to top seeds Switzerland, to pulling back from the brink against Poland with three quick goals in the last 12 minutes to win 3-2, then beating Albania 2-1 on the last day as the Swiss dropped points in Poland. "We've done it the hard way, but we've shown great maturity and determination to succeed," declared Kerr as her joyful players danced around the Loro Boriçi Stadium in Shkodër having secured a place at France 2019.

Kerr said she wanted to create a side that could "excite a nation" when she took over in 2017.

ONES TO WATCH

RACHEL CORSIE
Born: 17 August 1989
Position: Defender

Tore a cruciate ligament in 2012 but has worked her way back to surpass the 100-cap mark and is the current team captain. Enjoyed a silverware-laden six years with Scottish champions Glasgow City and has since carved out a successful career in the National Women's Soccer League in the USA with Seattle Reign FC and Utah Royals FC. An intelligent footballer, she holds the UEFA B Licence and is a stylish and calm presence in Scotland's backline and can play in midfield if needed.

KIM LITTLE
Born: 29 June 1990
Position: Midfielder

The beating heart of Scotland's midfield, she was sorely missed when she suffered a cruciate ligament injury seven weeks before EURO 2017. Captain of Arsenal and vice-captain of Scotland, she returned to international duty during qualification to score and create crucial goals. A technical and visionary footballer with a winning mentality, she has been key to league triumphs at Hibernian, Seattle Reign FC, Melbourne City FC and Arsenal. World class in every respect.

ERIN CUTHBERT
Born: 19 July 1998
Position: Forward

Accompanied her hero Julie Fleeting as a Scotland mascot as a child and has become a role model in her own right with some vital performances for her country. Four days after her 19th birthday she swept in a beauty against Portugal at EURO 2017 to become the first woman to score for Scotland in a major tournament. Tore teams apart in qualifying with her speed, skill and goals. Plays professionally for Chelsea in the FA Women's Super League and will be a handful for any defence in France.

WOMEN'S WORLD CUP RECORD

After missing out in the play-offs for the FIFA Women's World Cup 2015, debutants Scotland made sure of their ticket to this year's finals by topping their group on the last day of qualifying.

Scotland have done that, their 2-1 win over Switzerland in August 2018 attracting a record 4,098 fans, their qualification feat setting Twitter alight.

It has helped that professionals dominate the squad, most playing in England, others in America, Italy and Sweden. Perhaps more excitingly, the team we see in France this summer will all have trained full time in 2019 after the Scottish government decided to fund Kerr's home-based players ahead of the tournament. Get ready then, to watch the fittest, most technically skilled Scotland side yet.

Left: Vice-captain Kim Little has won silverware on three continents.

ARGENTINA

Inspirational underdogs are already winners

Thrown into tough groups in both of their previous FIFA Women's World Cup™ appearances, Argentina were unable to get off the ground in either. Will *La Albiceleste* make their presence felt the third time around?

THE COACH

CARLOS BORRELLO

Boasts a long association with the national side, having first taken the head coach job with responsibility for all age groups back in 1998. Won plaudits as Argentina rose in the world ranking on his watch and beat Brazil to win their first-ever *Copa América Femenina* title in 2006. Has bags of major tournament experience after reaching two consecutive FIFA Women's World Cups and an Olympic Games with the seniors. Left in 2012 and enjoyed domestic success in the *Primera División*, winning silverware with UAI Urquiza before rejoining the national side in 2017 and leading them to France against the odds.

Above: Argentina celebrate as one after reaching France 2019.

SUCCESS IN FRANCE would certainly be a shot in the arm for the national team and the women's game in a country where men's football dominates. Having said that, even reaching this summer's tournament has won Carlos Borrello's players widespread respect.

That is because Argentina, ranked in the top 30 in the world in 2007 when they last made it to the FIFA Women's World Cup, achieved qualification despite a two-year hiatus during which they played no fixtures, had no coach and fell out of the world ranking.

The women's programme resumed in July 2017 and, apart from a brief player strike over conditions and pay, the experienced Borrello and his

group have spent the intervening period making up for lost time. That they were able to hold their own in the *Copa América Femenina* nine months later says much for the talent in their ranks and their determination to achieve.

With qualification for France 2019 as well as the Pan American Games at stake, the pressure to succeed was high. With just one loss in four group games, however, Argentina kept their nerve and made it into the final phase, where a 3-1 win over Colombia secured third place even with subsequent defeats to Brazil and hosts Chile.

That left *La Albiceleste* facing a play-off with Panama in November for one joint Concacaf/CONMEBOL spot at this FIFA Women's World

ONES TO WATCH

FLORENCIA BONSEGUNDO
Born: 14 July 1993
Position: Midfielder

A great character and leader with masterful set-piece technique who has bagged goals at two *Copa América Femenina* tournaments and the Pan American Games, where she scored a super free kick against Mexico on her 22nd birthday. Hit four goals in qualifying including a crucial effort against Panama in the away leg of their crunch play-off. "Flor" will look to kick on again in France and will arrive at the tournament having tasted European football after joining Spain's Sporting Huelva in 2018.

ESTEFANÍA BANINI
Born: 21 June 1990
Position: Midfielder/Forward

A versatile playmaker with great close control and goalscoring prowess, "La Messi" is an inspirational figure with vast overseas experience. Crowned women's footballer of the year during a silverware-laden spell with Chilean side Colo-Colo. Switched to Washington Spirit in the USA in 2015 and overcame an injury-hit debut season to win the Spirit Golden Boot the following year. Has also enjoyed spells in the Spanish top-flight with Valencia CF in 2016 and on loan with their city neighbours Levante UD in 2018.

SOLEDAD JAIMES
Born: 20 January 1989
Position: Forward

Crowd-pleasing "Sole" strikes terror into the hearts of defenders with her boundless energy, aerial power and clinical finishing. Hit five goals in the *Copa América Femenina* 2018 including a key effort against Colombia in the battle to reach France 2019. Has played for Santos in Brazil where her tally of 18 goals in 19 games in 2017 saw her become the second woman after Brazil legend Formiga to win the prestigious *Bola de Prata* award. Joined Olympique Lyonnais in 2019 from Dalian Quanjian.

Above: Skilful playmaker Estefanía Banini is known as Argentina's "female Messi".

WOMEN'S WORLD CUP RECORD

Year	Venue	Result
1991	China PR	Did not enter
1995	Sweden	Did not qualify
1999	USA	Did not qualify
2003	USA	Group stage (4th, Group C)
2007	China PR	Group stage (4th, Group A)
2011	Germany	Did not qualify
2015	Canada	Did not qualify

Cup. It was a make-or-break week and with improved backing from their association and friendlies in the USA and Puerto Rico in the run-up, Argentina were raring to go.

Roared on at the stadium of Arsenal de Sarandí by 11,500 fans, including several of Argentina's players from the unofficial Women's World Cup in 1971, Borrello's charges won 4-0. A 1-1 draw in the return leg in Panama City saw them through, a remarkable achievement indeed from a group of players whose focus now will be to go again on the pitches of France.

JAPAN

Slick, speedy and set to shine once more

Champions in 2011 and beaten finalists four years ago, can the *Nadeshiko* hit the heights again in 2019? Whatever happens, a revitalised Japan will give it their all.

Above: An elated Japan retained their AFC Women's Asian Cup crown in 2018.

LED BY FORMER midfielder Asako Takakura since 2016 and with a host of new faces in the squad, the side we see this summer will have evolved since Japan lit up the last two tournaments. That said, the speedy, slick passing game that is Japan's trademark style should still be in evidence in this, the nation's eighth successive FIFA Women's World Cup™ appearance.

Japan certainly revealed glimpses of their potential on the road to France as Takakura blooded new players and nurtured her veterans in a bid to revamp the senior side, suffering losses as well as big wins in the process.

Of course, the result that really mattered came in the AFC Women's Asian Cup, which acted as the qualifying tournament for this FIFA Women's World Cup. Eight

players from Japan's Canada 2015 exploits were among Takakura's 23-strong squad for that clash of confederation giants in April 2018 and despite losing out on top spot to Australia in the group stage, the Japanese secured qualification for France 2019 by reaching the semi-finals, where they beat China PR 3-1. The icing on the cake was a thrilling final victory over Australia a day after Takakura's 50th birthday. Just as pleasing for the coach as that late present was the feeling that her team had played the "*Nadeshiko* way".

Takakura went on to use the summer of 2018 to test new formations, challenge players to try different positions and give debuts to untried youngsters. With three straight losses to the USA, Brazil and Australia in the Tournament

THE COACH

ASAKO TAKAKURA

The first female coach of Japan, former international Asako Takakura boasts a fine pedigree having scored 30 goals for her country in 79 appearances, including at two FIFA Women's World Cups and an Olympic Games. Began coaching with the Japan Football Association in 2007 and as a youth coach won the AFC U-16 Women's Championship 2013, FIFA U-17 Women's World Cup 2014 and AFC U-19 Women's Championship 2015. A bold, tactically astute manager, she has been voted the AFC Women's Coach of the Year six times and is viewed in Japan as a true pioneer of the game.

ONES TO WATCH

SAKI KUMAGAI
Born: 17 October 1990
Position: Defender

Has stood up to be counted for club and country, scoring the trophy-winning penalty against the USA in the FIFA Women's World Cup 2011 and repeating the trick for Olympique Lyonnais against VfL Wolfsburg in the UEFA Women's Champions League final in 2016. Scored from the spot again in 2017 as Lyon beat Paris Saint-Germain on penalties to retain their European title. A versatile player who is equally at home in defence or midfield, she is an inspirational captain for Japan.

MANA IWABUCHI
Born: 18 March 1993
Position: Forward

Still only 26 but vastly experienced having played in Germany for TSG 1899 Hoffenheim and Bayern Munich, and for Japan at the FIFA Women's World Cup in both 2011 and 2015 as well as at the 2012 Olympics. Her breathtaking dribbling skills can set any match alight. Returned to Japan in 2017 to play for INAC Kobe Leonessa with a view to returning to full fitness after two injury-hit seasons in Germany. Her plan worked and she dominated the AFC Women's Asian Cup 2018 and was crowned most valuable player.

KUMI YOKOYAMA
Born: 13 August 1993
Position: Forward

Dubbed the "Japanese Maradona" in 2010 after beating five Korea DPR defenders to score a FIFA Puskas Award-nominated wondergoal in the semi-finals of the FIFA U-17 Women's World Cup. A diminutive but tenacious trickster and natural finisher who has overseas club experience with German side 1.FFC Frankfurt. Bagged four goals in the AFC Women's Asian Cup 2018, including the winner against Australia, and will hope to make a difference again this summer.

Above: Former youth star Mana Iwabuchi is a mainstay for Japan.

WOMEN'S WORLD CUP RECORD

Year	Venue	Result
1991	China PR	Group stage (4th, Group B)
1995	Sweden	Quarter-finalists
1999	USA	Group stage (4th, Group C)
2003	USA	Group stage (3rd, Group C)
2007	China PR	Group stage (3rd, Group A)
2011	Germany	Winners
2015	Canada	Runners-up

of Nations swiftly followed by an unbeaten title-winning Asian Games campaign, the results were certainly mixed.

Even so, the players emerged from this period united in their determination to prove their status as among the world's best. The *Young Nadeshiko* did so when they won the FIFA U-20 Women's World Cup in France last summer – making Japan the only nation to have won women's world titles at every age group – and now it is the turn of this revamped senior side to step up.

GROUP E

Paired together for the second finals running, European champions the Netherlands and top seeds Canada meet again on the last day of group action on 20 June in Reims. The battle for supremacy could go to the wire then, especially if Cameroon and Oceania champions New Zealand can reprise their qualification form.

Main: *Montpellier's Stade de la Mosson on the south coast of France was one of the venues for the 1998 FIFA World Cup™.*

Montpellier

🍁 CANADA

Olympians gear up to go again on world stage

As hosts, Canada played their part in the record-breaking FIFA Women's World Cup 2015™, but there was no dream podium finish on home soil. Now the *Canucks* return with a new coach and renewed vigour.

Above: Canada are one of the teams to watch at France 2019.

IF CANADA'S WOMEN were disappointed by their sixth-place finish on the world stage four years ago, they did not let it hold them back. At Rio 2016, they celebrated a second consecutive Olympic bronze after a stunning 2-1 win over Brazil, rising to their highest world ranking of fourth as a result.

The *Canucks* had to rally again in 2017 as a host of veterans, including influential players Melissa Tancredi and Rhian Wilkinson, retired from international football. Then, as the new year dawned, the squad were hit by the revelation that their manager of six years, John Herdman, was leaving to take charge of Canada's men.

To the credit of both the players and the Englishman's immediate replacement, Kenneth Heiner-Møller, they stayed calm and got on with the job in hand, which was to ready themselves for the upcoming qualifying campaign for France 2019 via the Concacaf Women's Championship in October 2018.

Beginning the new era with a 3-1 defeat at the hands of Sweden in the Algarve Cup was not ideal, but Canada bowed out in fifth place after a decisive 2-0 win over Japan. Narrow friendly losses to France and Germany followed, but Heiner-Møller was experimenting with formations by this stage, and a 1-0 win over Brazil in September indicated progress.

A month later, a squad that included five teenagers but was missing injured stalwarts Erin McLeod and Desiree Scott came good for the

THE COACH

KENNETH HEINER-MØLLER
Won a league and cup double in 1995 as a player with Hungarian side Ferencváros and ten years later as the coach of Danish women's team Brøndby IF. Became Denmark women's national team head coach the following year and led them at the FIFA Women's World Cup 2007 and at two UEFA Women's EUROs, reaching the semi-finals in 2013. Joined Canada in 2015 as an assistant coach under John Herdman and helped deliver the bronze-medal win at Rio 2016. Took over the top job in January 2018 and will use all his experience and football nous to take the *Canucks* to another level.

ONES TO WATCH

JESSIE FLEMING
Born: 11 March 1998
Position: Midfielder

Canada's female U-20 player of the year three times running, this UCLA Bruins star is now a regular for the seniors after making her international debut aged 15. Played 80 minutes at the FIFA Women's World Cup 2015 and now, aged 21, already has that experience, an Olympic bronze medal and more than half a century of caps in her locker. A playmaker with lightning-quick reactions and super technique, she should relish a return to the world stage.

SOPHIE SCHMIDT
Born: 28 June 1988
Position: Midfielder

Another player who made her Canada debut as a teenager, this midfield maestro played in a remarkable 76 consecutive internationals between 2011 and 2015. She was virtually ever-present at Canada 2015, earning praise from FIFA's panel of experts for her tactical acumen, leadership and fighting mentality. Plays with simplicity and spirit and has honed her talent through more than 175 appearances for Canada along with spells at Kristianstads DFF in Sweden, Sky Blue FC in the USA and 1.FFC Frankfurt in Germany.

CHRISTINE SINCLAIR
Born: 12 June 1983
Position: Forward

Captain, legend, goal-getter, Portland Thorns striker "Sincy" watched the FIFA Women's World Cup 1999 as a teenage fan and played for Canada on the international stage herself the following year aged just 16. Made her FIFA Women's World Cup debut in 2003 and earned her 270th cap during France 2019 qualifying, scoring her 177th international goal in the process. Now playing a slightly deeper role, with her imposing physical presence and phenomenal strike rate, she remains a guiding light for the *Canucks*.

Above: Christine SInclair scored her first FIFA Women's World Cup goal in 2003.

WOMEN'S WORLD CUP RECORD

Year	Venue	Result
1991	China PR	Did not qualify
1995	Sweden	Group stage (3rd, Group B)
1999	USA	Group stage (3rd, Group C)
2003	USA	Fourth place
2007	China PR	Group stage (3rd, Group C)
2011	Germany	Group stage (4th, Group A)
2015	Canada	Quarter-finalists

most crucial test of all, the Concacaf Women's Championship. A medal finish and a place at this summer's finals were at stake and after victories over Jamaica, Cuba, Costa Rica and Panama, it was mission accomplished.

Losing 2-0 in a feisty final against the USA suggested there was room for improvement. Still, with so many youthful talents emerging, top-class veterans with so much to give and maturing stars Kadeisha Buchanan, Jessie Fleming and Rebecca Quinn staking their claims, Canada might make that podium finish yet.

CAMEROON

Can *Les Lionnes* prove indomitable in France?

Returning for their second consecutive finals appearance, Cameroon were the only African side to progress past the group stage at Canada 2015 and their positive play should once again prove a challenge for any opponents.

FOUR YEARS AGO, *Les Lionnes* won the hearts of neutrals with their exuberant attacking style, choreographed goal celebrations and some colourful hairdos. They won games too, defeating fellow debutants Ecuador 6-0 and coming from behind to beat Switzerland 2-1. China PR knocked them out 1-0 in the round of 16 but they had demonstrated that they belonged at this level.

The core of the squad has remained constant since the London 2012 Olympics, with an ever-increasing number of players leaving Cameroon to earn a living from the game. At the time of the Women's Africa Cup of Nations 2018 in Ghana, which served as the qualifiers for this summer's world finals, 16 were based in Europe, nine of them in France. As a consequence, a crucial challenge for coach Joseph Brian Ndoko is ensuring cohesion on the field between overseas and locally based players, though that ongoing conundrum did not prevent them making it to France.

Les Lionnes received a bye in the first round of qualifying for Ghana 2018 and swept past Congo in the second round in June before beating Mali and Algeria and drawing with the hosts at the tournament proper in November.

Topping Group A teed up a clash with their "nemesis" Nigeria in the last four. Cameroon had lost the previous two finals to the *Super Falcons* and the 1-0 defeat two years

Below: Les Lionnes *will look to make Africa proud and progress to the knockout stage once more.*

THE COACH

JOSEPH BRIAN NDOKO
Took over *Les Lionnes* in June 2017 having previously managed Aigle Royal de la Menoua in the Cameroonian men's first division. He succeeded Carl Enow Ngachu, who had been in charge for more than a decade and was one of the longest-serving coaches in African women's football. This is Ndoko's first foray into the women's game but he is assisted by the side's former captain Bernadette Anong, who has worked with the team since 2014. "We failed at the Women's Africa Cup of Nations because we dropped our level of play," he says, "but it is our target to get out of the group at the World Cup again."

ONES TO WATCH

CHRISTINE MANIE
Born: 4 May 1984
Position: Defender

An experienced centre-back and the team's captain. Scored vital goals in qualifying for both London 2012 and Canada 2015. Calm from the spot and brave in the air, she has netted in successive continental finals and won gold at the All Africa Games in 2011. Played in Belarus and then in Romania, where she won four league titles with Olimpia Cluj and competed in the UEFA Women's Champions League. Has since been at French second-division side AS Nancy.

GAËLLE ENGANAMOUIT
Born: 9 June 1992
Position: Forward

A powerful and strong-running forward. Struck a hat-trick on her country's FIFA Women's World Cup™ debut, a 6-0 win over Ecuador at Canada 2015. She also top-scored in Sweden for Eskilstuna United DFF and collected the 2015 African Women's Player of the Year award to complete a stellar year. A serious knee injury virtually wrote off the following season with FC Rosengård and her 2017 season in China PR was injury-affected too, but she regained form with Avaldsnes in Norway in 2018.

GABRIELLE ONGUÉNÉ
Born: 25 February 1989
Position: Forward

An enterprising player who torments defenders on the right side of attack and thrills crowds with her speed, skill and opportunism. Won the Russian title with WFC Rossiyanka in 2016 and the cup with CSKA Moscow the following year. An impressively consistent performer for *Les Lionnes* and the scorer of the team's only goal at London 2012, she was the player of the tournament at the Women's Africa Cup of Nations 2016 and shortlisted for African Women's Player of the Year three years running.

Above: When fit and in form, Gaëlle Enganamouit is a bona fide goal machine.

WOMEN'S WORLD CUP RECORD

Year	Venue	Result
1991	China PR	Did not qualify
1995	Sweden	Did not enter
1999	USA	Did not qualify
2003	USA	Did not qualify
2007	China PR	Did not qualify
2011	Germany	Did not qualify
2015	Canada	Round of 16

earlier had been a particularly painful one, as it was on home soil, in front of a sell-out crowd of over 40,000 in Yaoundé. Alas, a lively semi-final this time around ended 0-0 and the tie was decided by a shoot-out in which Nigeria prevailed against their rivals for the 12th time in the continental finals. The side refocused for the third-place match, though, and fired their way to a 4-2 victory against Mali to secure the final African spot at France 2019.

Boasting an explosive front three of Ajara Nchout, Gabrielle Onguéné and Gaëlle Enganamouit, *Les Lionnes* were a hit with fans in 2015. Expect further entertainment in France this summer.

NEW ZEALAND

Fresh start for *Football Ferns* as they head to France

Yet to record a victory at the FIFA Women's World Cup™, New Zealand will be looking to make history this summer. They qualified with ease; can they transfer their continental dominance to the world stage?

Above: Oceania champions New Zealand were untouchable in qualifying.

NEW ZEALAND were the last team to throw their hat into the ring for France 2019 and, although they were favourites to qualify via the OFC Women's Nations Cup in December 2018, they did so in style with a winning run that included 43 goals for and none conceded.

It was a happy end to a tumultuous period for the *Football Ferns* that began in November 2017 with the unexpected resignation of popular head coach of six years, Tony Readings. A collective bargaining agreement securing the same pay, prize money and travel as the men's team, and news that the domestic league was to be expanded were fillips the following May, but a bullying row involving new head coach Andreas Heraf led to an independent review and his resignation in July.

The *Ferns* finally got back on track in October 2018 when New Zealand Football apologised to the players and the experienced Tom Sermanni was installed as head coach. With the OFC Women's Nations Cup looming, the team needed to regroup quickly and they did, retaining their continental crown and taking Oceania's only spot at France 2019 and the 2020 Olympics in the process.

Pleasingly for Sermanni, Sarah Gregorius was on fire with eight goals, while exciting youngsters such as winger Paige Satchell and midfielder Grace Jale had blended brilliantly with an experienced squad featuring 11 overseas-based players and centurions Betsy Hassett, Annalie Longo, Ria Percival and skipper Ali Riley.

If a winning start for the new

THE COACH

TOM SERMANNI

Popular and easy-going, Glasgow-born Sermanni has a wealth of experience in the women's game. A veteran of three FIFA Women's World Cups as head coach, he got his first taste of the competition with Australia in 1995 and led the *Matildas* to the quarter-finals in 2007 and 2011 during a second stint that lasted almost eight years. Managed the USA women's national team in 2013 and 2014 before joining Canada's programme as an assistant to former New Zealand boss John Herdman. Most recently worked with the likes of Brazil star Marta and USA hotshot Alex Morgan at Orlando Pride in the NWSL.

ONES TO WATCH

ERIN NAYLER
Born: 17 April 1992
Position: Goalkeeper

Rarely tested in qualifying but regarded as a top keeper who reads the game well and is capable of facing down the best opponents with her great aerial strength, smart distribution and strong communication. Shone for the *Football Ferns* at the last FIFA Women's World Cup and now boasts even more experience after winning over half a century of caps. Will relish the chance to play on the world stage in France, having played for Grenoble, before becoming number 1 for Bordeaux.

RIA PERCIVAL
Born: 7 December 1989
Position: Defender

A free-kick specialist who loves to power forward, take opponents on and pick out team-mates with trademark long-range passes. She made her senior debut in 2006 aged 16 and surpassed Abby Erceg's record of 132 caps for New Zealand during France 2019 qualifying. A consummate professional, she has vast experience of different styles of football having played for clubs in America, Canada, Germany and Switzerland. Born in England, she returned to her roots in 2018 when she joined FA Women's Super League side West Ham United.

ROSIE WHITE
Born: 6 June 1993
Position: Forward

Underwent surgery to treat stress fractures in both feet in early 2018 but had a spring in her step during qualifying, scoring six goals and finishing just shy of a century of caps. Strong, versatile and capable, she was a consistent performer for Boston Breakers in the NWSL before joining Chicago Red Stars in 2018. Her start was delayed by injury, but she impressed enough from midfield to land a contract extension and will surely have benefited from playing alongside the likes of Australian superstar Sam Kerr.

Above: Stalwart Ria Percival is New Zealand's record cap holder.

WOMEN'S WORLD CUP RECORD

Year	Venue	Result
1991	China PR	Group stage (4th, Group A)
1995	Sweden	Did not qualify
1999	USA	Did not qualify
2003	USA	Did not qualify
2007	China PR	Group stage (4th, Group D
2011	Germany	Group stage (4th, Group B)
2015	Canada	Group stage (4th, Group A)

Sermanni era was a moment to savour, it tasted even sweeter a few hours later when the squad excitedly watched live footage of the *Junior Football Ferns* winning bronze at the FIFA U-17 Women's World Cup, New Zealand's first FIFA tournament medal. The seniors need just one victory to make history of their own in France and with Sermanni's nous together with their own mental strength and talent, they ought to achieve that target and much more.

THE NETHERLANDS

Champions of Europe are eyeing another crown

The *Oranje Leeuwinnen* may have again required the play-offs to qualify for their second FIFA Women's World Cup™ but the way the UEFA Women's EURO 2017 winners perform under pressure surely makes them contenders in France.

THE COACH

SARINA WIEGMAN

A former national team captain, she became the first Dutch player to reach 100 caps in 2001. Played a season at the University of North Carolina alongside USA legends Mia Hamm and Kristine Lilly and worked as a teacher during her successful club career in the Netherlands. She retired in 2003, managing her old side Ter Leede then ADO Den Haag before rejoining the *Oranje Leeuwinnen* as assistant in 2014. On the staff at Canada 2015 and caretaker boss twice, she was appointed head coach in January 2017 with the team at a low ebb and just six months before hosting a home EURO which they sensationally won. Named The Best FIFA Women's Coach 2017.

Above: Elation for Oranje Leeuwinnen *after their play-off success versus Switzerland.*

EN ROUTE to winning their first major trophy two years ago, the Netherlands displayed defensive discipline, expansive attacking flair and tremendous mental strength. The summer of 2017 witnessed a women's football revolution as the host team's performances and their joyous support reached a crescendo in Enschede with a 4-2 title-winning victory over Denmark. Over 28,000 fans packed the stands that day and excitingly, the legacy of that success and their popularity continued throughout the following qualifying campaign, though it would take four extra matches for them to reach France 2019.

Beating Norway 1-0 was a solid start but their campaign derailed slightly when the Republic of Ireland withstood an intense bombardment to hold out for a goalless draw in Nijmegen in November 2017. As a consequence, despite winning the matches that followed, they needed at least a draw in the last game away to Norway but fell frustratingly short, losing 2-1.

For the second time in four years they were plunged into the play-offs, along with the other three best runners-up in the European zone, to compete for the last, prized berth. Drawn to play Denmark in the semi-finals, they breezily dismissed the EURO 2017 finalists 4-1 on aggregate. Switzerland had pipped Belgium on away goals in the other semi but they were no match for the Dutch in the final. Tickets for the

ONES TO WATCH

JACKIE GROENEN
Born: 17 December 1994
Position: Midfielder

Has matured into a highly effective link between defence and attack and rarely wastes possession. Won national titles and a European medal in judo but stopped competing at 16. Represented the Netherlands at youth level and had a later request to switch to play for Belgium, where she grew up, turned down. A law student at Tilburg University, she has played most of her club career in Germany, though she spent 2014-15 with Chelsea in England. Included in the EURO 2017 team of the tournament.

LIEKE MARTENS
Born: 16 December 1992
Position: Midfielder/Forward

A supremely skilful left winger who loves to run at defenders and to cut inside onto her stronger right foot. Scored the first Dutch goal at a FIFA Women's World Cup in their 1-0 win over New Zealand in Canada. She was named player of the tournament at EURO 2017, UEFA Women's Player of the Year 2017 and then The Best FIFA Women's Player 2017 to complete the set. Joined FC Barcelona from Swedish side FC Rosengård in 2017. Started all 12 games for the Netherlands in qualifying.

VIVIANNE MIEDEMA
Born: 15 July 1996
Position: Forward

A goalscoring sensation whose languid style masks her potency. An intelligent user of space and movement to find dangerous positions or benefit team-mates. By the end of 2018 she had amassed 53 goals in just 68 appearances for the *Oranje Leeuwinnen* and the bigger the game, it seems, the more likely she is to register. Part of a Dutch quartet at Arsenal, having moved to England from Bayern Munich in 2017. Is the co-author of a series of children's books.

Above: The star of the UEFA Women's EURO 2017, can Lieke Martens make a similar impact in France?

WOMEN'S WORLD CUP RECORD

Year	Venue	Result
1991	China PR	Did not qualify
1995	Sweden	Did not qualify
1999	USA	Did not qualify
2003	USA	Did not qualify
2007	China PR	Did not qualify
2011	Germany	Did not qualify
2015	Canada	Round of 16

tie in Utrecht sold out in less than half an hour and in front of 23,750 fans, the highest attendance for any European women's play-off, the Dutch sizzled to a 3-0 win. Despite captain Anouk Dekker's early red in the return leg, Vivianne Miedema's strike was enough for a 1-1 draw.

They exited their first FIFA Women's World Cup in the second round, losing 2-1 to eventual finalists Japan, but viewed it as a positive learning experience. This talented outfit, consisting of players based at top professional sides across Europe, know what it takes to be champions. Get ready for *Oranjegekte* to sweep across France.

GROUP F

Current title-holders the USA and their perennial finals opponents Sweden are tipped for success in a group featuring two of the world's rising football nations. A learning curve for Chile and Thailand perhaps, but who will come out on top after the Americans and Swedes have slugged it out in Le Havre on 20 June?

Main: Formerly known as the Stade de la Route de Lorient, Roazhon Park in Rennes was originally built in 1912 and will accommodate 29,820 spectators at France 2019.

 # USA

The world's best are ready to take on the rest

The USA secured a first FIFA Women's World Cup™ title in 16 years when they vanquished Japan 5-2 in the final at Canada 2015. Can they retain their crown in similar style in France?

THE COACH

JILL ELLIS
Followed her father into coaching and achieved considerable success with college side UCLA Bruins. Began her association with the national set-up as U-21 coach in 2000 and went on to assist former head coach Pia Sundhage as they led the seniors to Olympic gold in 2008 and 2012. Having twice served as interim head coach, the 52-year-old accepted the top job in spring 2014 and by the following summer had led the USA to a first FIFA Women's World Cup title since 1999. Will be under pressure out in France but is capable of rising to the challenge.

Above: Concacaf champions the USA cruised to qualification for France 2019.

THE ARCHITECT OF THE USA's third FIFA Women's World Cup triumph, head coach Jill Ellis, will certainly expect so after overseeing a tricky period of transition and coming out the other side with a thrilling squad that are hard to beat.

It was always going to be a tall order to replace inspirational skipper Christie Rampone, classy midfielders Lauren Holiday, Shannon Boxx and Heather O'Reilly, and the world's top goalscorer Abby Wambach, who all hung up their international boots after Canada 2015. Indeed, after suffering a crushing penalty shoot-out loss to Sweden in the quarter-finals of the Olympics in 2016, it almost looked an impossible job.

However, England-born Ellis, who has almost two decades of experience with the national set-up, responded positively, dabbling with formations, assessing her established players and blooding new ones. Remarkably, between Rio and the USA's own elite four-team invitational SheBelieves Cup in 2018 – which they won – Ellis had run the rule over more than 50 players in training camps and given 15 their first cap.

By October 2018, a blend of Canada 2015 champions and newer talents had retained the USA's Concacaf Women's Championship crown, delivering qualification for France 2019 along the way. The USA then closed out the year with a friendly tour of Europe where

ONES TO WATCH

ROSE LAVELLE
Born: 14 May 1995
Position: Midfielder

Ever-present in the USA's run to the quarter-finals of the FIFA U-20 Women's World Cup in 2014, this former college soccer star made an impressive senior debut against England in the 2017 SheBelieves Cup. Her progress was hit by a long injury lay-off but she has picked up where she left off, starring for Washington Spirit in the NWSL and her national side in 2018. A tricky dribbler with nimble feet who loves to nutmeg opponents, she is tipped for big things in 2019 and beyond.

LINDSEY HORAN
Born: 26 May 1994
Position: Midfielder/Forward

Made the bold move to join Paris Saint-Germain in 2012, becoming the first American woman to sign professional terms straight from high school. Went on to hit 46 goals in 58 league matches for the French club and gained UEFA Women's Champions League experience in the process. Similarly influential for Portland Thorns in the NWSL and the national side since her return to the USA in 2016, she was last season's NWSL most valuable player and is a versatile, popular and stylish footballer.

ALEX MORGAN
Born: 2 July 1989
Position: Forward

A fast, determined and fearless forward who has proved her world-class credentials with goals in two Olympics and two FIFA Women's World Cups. Has played for Portland Thorns and Orlando Pride in the NWSL and enjoyed a successful loan spell with French giants Olympique Lyonnais in 2017, winning the league, French Cup and UEFA Women's Champions League. The Golden Boot winner at the Concacaf qualifying tournament, by the close of 2018 she had amassed an impressive 98 goals in 153 international appearances.

Above: Worla-class forward Alex Morgan boasts a truly impressive goal tally.

WOMEN'S WORLD CUP RECORD

Year	Venue	Result
1991	China PR	Winners
1995	Sweden	Third place
1999	USA	Winners
2003	USA	Third place
2007	China PR	Third place
2011	Germany	Runners-up
2015	Canada	Winners

they beat Portugal 1-0 to record a 500th win for the national team, before edging Scotland by the same scoreline. All told, they had won 18 games, drawn twice and scored 65 goals over the previous 12 months.

Julie Ertz, Alex Morgan, Megan Rapinoe, Becky Sauerbrunn and two-time FIFA Women's World Player of the Year Carli Lloyd continue to underpin the squad, but Ellis has brought some gems to the fore too in Tierna Davidson, Lindsey Horan, Rose Lavelle, Mallory Pugh and Emily Sonnett amongst others.

Whoever makes the cut, the entire group will arrive in France united in their aim to retain their status as number one in the world.

THAILAND

Can the *Chaba Kaew* reach the knockout phase this time?

Standard-bearers of the developing women's game in Southeast Asia, the region's most successful side are back on the biggest stage and aiming to avoid another early exit at their second FIFA Women's World Cup™.

THAILAND WERE BEATEN 4-0 by both Norway and Germany in the group stage in Canada but there was cause for celebration when they registered a historic 3-2 maiden tournament win over fellow debutants Côte d'Ivoire. Four years later, with a similar squad but greater experience and belief, they will proudly return as one of the 24 elite sides in the competition this summer.

Thailand have won the last three editions of Southeast Asia's AFF Women's Championship and facing Palestine and Chinese Taipei in qualification for the AFC Women's Asian Cup 2018 proved no object. However, with only five places at France 2019 up for grabs, the next phase in Asian qualifying posed a tougher challenge.

Losing to China PR was not an ideal start to their finals campaign but they rallied with triumphs over hosts Jordan and the Philippines. The latter result saw them into the final four for the first time in 32 years and also confirmed their ticket to France.

In the semi-finals they pushed the much higher-ranked Australia all the way. Behind to an early own goal, Kanjana Sung-Ngoen's speed on the counter-attack terrorised the *Matildas'* defence and her lob levelled the game before Rattikan Thongsombut put them 2-1 ahead. Agonisingly for Nuengruethai Sathongwien's determined side, Australia equalised in stoppage time and went on to win 3-1 in the

Below: Thailand may not be the strongest Asian side at France 2019, but they are always proud and purposeful opponents.

THE COACH

NUENGRUETHAI SATHONGWIEN Previously working in club football and initially brought in as national team assistant in 2013. Holds the distinctions of being the side's first female head coach and the only manager to have steered a Thai team to a senior FIFA World Cup finals, a pioneering feat she can now boast to have achieved twice. Stepped down into a supporting role after losing to Vietnam in the second round of the AFC Women's Olympic Qualifying Tournament for Rio 2016 but retook the reins when her replacement, former English Premier League defender Spencer Prior, resigned in September 2017.

ONES TO WATCH

SILAWAN INTAMEE
Born: 22 January 1994
Position: Midfielder

From the beautiful Chiang Mai province in the north of the country. Played every minute at Canada 2015, despite being the second-youngest member of the squad. She has a slight frame but immense energy and pulls the strings in central midfield. Her left foot regularly conjures up chances and contributes goals from set pieces. "I've been working very hard on practising free kicks," she revealed after scoring cute curling efforts against both Jordan and the Philippines during qualification for France 2019.

TANEEKARN DANGDA
Born: 15 December 1992
Position: Forward

A tall and skilful left-sided forward whose childhood dream of becoming a model came true when she competed in Thailand's Supermodel Contest in 2015. Her father played football for the the Royal Thai Air Force, while she is also inspired by her older brother Teerasil, a star of the men's national team. She was an unused member of the squad in Canada but started every game at the AFC Women's Asian Cup 2018 and netted in the 6-1 defeat of hosts Jordan in the group stage.

KANJANA SUNG-NGOEN
Born: 21 September 1986
Position: Forward

The team's go-to player possesses strength and blistering pace. Most often found marauding down the right but able to operate on either flank or in the striker's role. The scorer of both goals in the celebrated 2-1 victory over Vietnam in 2014, which secured the *Chaba Kaew*'s first-ever FIFA Women's World Cup finals appearance, she also struck four times at Jordan 2018, meaning she has now scored 44 per cent of her country's goals at the past two AFC Women's Asian Cups.

penalty shoot-out. They may have fallen 3-1 to China PR in the play-off for third place, but Thailand's main objective had been achieved and the team were greeted by crowds of admiring fans on their return to Bangkok.

Defeats to Finland, Portugal and again to hosts China PR in an invitational competition in October 2018 indicate there is work to be done. The Thai Women's Premier League has been largely inactive since 2013 although the national squad trains together and plays regularly. Thailand will be tricky adversaries, though, and are not to be taken lightly.

Above: *Capable of breakneck speed, Kanjana Sung-Ngoen remains a leading light for the Chaba Kaew.*

WOMEN'S WORLD CUP RECORD

Year	Venue	Result
1991	China PR	Did not qualify
1995	Sweden	Did not enter
1999	USA	Did not enter
2003	USA	Did not qualify
2007	China PR	Did not qualify
2011	Germany	Did not qualify
2015	Canada	Group stage (3rd, Group B)

CHILE

South American first-timers living their dream

Cheered on by home fans, *La Roja* finished second at the *Copa América Femenina 2018* to secure a spot at their first FIFA Women's World Cup™. Can they continue to surprise?

THE COACH

JOSÉ LETELIER

A goalkeeper in his youth, José Letelier won the *Copa Libertadores* as a squad member with Santiago-based side Colo-Colo in 1991, a feat he repeated as coach of the club's women's team 21 years later. He hung up his gloves in 1997 and soon moved into coaching. Graduated from Colo-Colo's youth teams to the *Femenino* team in 2010, leading them to multiple titles. Took charge of the Chile women's U-20s in 2015 and then the senior *La Roja* in 2016. The players know him well and he communicates his ideas clearly – crucial elements in the team's excellent organisation.

Above: Jubilation for La Roja *as they beat Argentina to book their spot in France.*

COPA AMÉRICA FEMININA RUNNERS-UP just once before in 1991, the underdog hosts started slowly in the opening stages of the tournament in April 2018. Following 1-1 draws with Paraguay and Colombia, *La Roja* dominated against Uruguay but required a María José Rojas finish in the 80th minute to earn their first win. After finding their groove, they pummelled Peru 5-0 to finish second in Group A.

Despite losing 3-1 to Brazil in the opening game of the final phase, they still wowed the crowd when Yesenia López scored from long range. Another stalemate with Colombia left them needing a win over Argentina, and in front of a rocking stadium, *La Roja* rose to the occasion to beat *La Albiceleste* 4-0,

clinching second place and their ticket to France.

José Letelier's determined squad are gaining experience and learning quickly, trips overseas to play the likes of USA and Australia all aiding their preparation. Often physically outmatched by the powerhouse nations, they play a low-pressing game, are tough to break down and possess ample technical ability. Most of the squad have left the *Campeonato Nacional* to play club football overseas, many in Spain.

Realistically, they have little prospect of lifting the trophy in France but simply playing competitive international fixtures must feel like a victory in itself.

Any optimism sparked by hosting the FIFA U-20 Women's World Cup

ONES TO WATCH

CHRISTIANE ENDLER
Born: 23 July 1991
Position: Goalkeeper

La Roja's captain and six-time Chilean player of the year. Born in Santiago, with a German father, she played outfield as a youngster and was inspired by the FIFA U-20 Women's World Cup 2008 to dedicate herself to football. "Tiane" has kept goal for Chilean sides Unión La Calera, Everton and Colo-Colo, as well as the University of South Florida. Signed for Chelsea in April 2014 but returned home with a knee injury. Joined Paris Saint-Germain from Valencia CF in 2017. The almost six-foot stopper is regarded as one of the world's best.

FRANCISCA LARA
Born: 29 July 1990
Position: Midfielder

Along with defender Carla Guerrero, "Pancha" is one of the side's most experienced outfield players and definitely one to watch. Former clubs include Ferroviarios, Coquimbo Unido, Cobreloa and then dominant domestic side Colo-Colo from 2012. A hugely versatile character with an eye for goal. Able to operate in defence, central midfield or on the left of the attack, where she impressed for Sporting Huelva, earning a transfer to fellow Spanish club Sevilla FC in the summer of 2018.

MARÍA JOSÉ ROJAS
Born: 17 December 1987
Position: Forward

Rapid, exciting, right-sided forward who starred for the University of Texas in San Antonio from 2010, then signed for Herforder SV in 2014 to become the first Chilean to play in Germany's *Frauen-Bundesliga*. Registered more intrepid firsts when featuring for Gintra-Universitetas of Lithuania in the UEFA Women's Champions League in 2017, before going on to turn out for Nadeshiko League Division 2 side Orca Kamogawa FC in Japan and Canberra United of Australia's W-League.

WOMEN'S WORLD CUP RECORD
Newcomers Chile set the *Copa América Femenina* alight in April 2018 when they beat Argentina 4-0 at home to book their debut FIFA Women's World Cup place.

in 2008 faded as support from the *Asociación Nacional de Fútbol Profesional* (ANFP) dwindled. *La Roja* did not play any fixtures from 2014 until May 2017 and plummeted in the FIFA Women's World Ranking from 38th to 137th.

With the assistance of the World Players' Union FIFPro, a Chilean women's players' association was formed in 2016. Dialogue with the authorities resumed, relations improved, Chile held the successful *Copa América Femenina* in April 2018 and a play-off against an African side will determine if they will attend the Tokyo 2020 Olympic Games too. The future looks rosy for *La Roja*.

Left: Chile's classy goalkeeper, captain and leader, Christiane Endler.

SWEDEN

Solid Sweden come seeking gold

Inaugural European champions in 1984, Sweden have consistently appeared on the world stage ever since but, despite being a "tournament team", silver medals are the best they have to show for it. So far.

THE COACH

PETER GERHARDSSON
Former forward and Swedish youth international who scored 49 top-flight goals for Hammarby IF in a playing career that spanned the late 1970s to the early 1990s, also working as a police officer during much of that period. Has coached both men's and women's teams, starting with hometown club Upsala IF in 1993 and most recently spending eight seasons at BK Häcken, where he clinched an *Allsvenskan* runners-up spot in 2012 and the 2016 Swedish Cup. He said it "felt like Christmas Eve" upon being appointed but having to wait eight months to succeed the legendary Pia Sundhage after the UEFA Women's EURO 2017.

Above: Sofia Jakobsson's team-mates rush to her after her goal against Denmark.

"A GOOD, CALM WIN," was the response of Sweden's happy coach Peter Gerhardsson as his team celebrated beating Denmark and securing qualification for the FIFA Women's World Cup™ France 2019, "I thought it would get a lot worse." It could have done after their surprise defeat three months earlier.

The *Blågult* kicked off their qualifying campaign in September 2017 by winning 2-0 in Croatia and a month later they were gifted three points and a 3-0 scoreline against Denmark, due to a then unresolved financial dispute between the UEFA Women's EURO 2017 finalists and their association.

Sweden appeared to be in total control of Group 4. The Rio 2016 silver medallists had also made the final at the 2018 Algarve Cup in March, though it was cancelled due to poor weather, and so their qualifying defeat in Lviv in June was a shock. Ukraine, who had lost 5-1 to Denmark days earlier, pressed well, defended solidly and Daryna Apanaschenko struck on a counter-attack for a 1-0 win that opened up the race for the lone automatic qualifying spot for France 2019.

In the end, everything rested on a final showdown across the Øresund Strait. Denmark needed a victory in Viborg to progress but it was Gerhardsson's side that grabbed the vital goal. In the first minute of the second half, Sofia Jakobsson latched onto Kosovare Asllani's ball forward and dispatched it precisely into the bottom corner. The *Blågult* had

ONES TO WATCH

NILLA FISCHER
Born: 2 August 1984
Position: Defender

Captained VfL Wolfsburg to back-to-back German league and cup doubles and was integral to their UEFA Women's Champions League success in 2014 and runs to the final in 2016 and 2018. Started playing football with her twin brother and earned most of her first 100 caps for Sweden as a combative midfielder before converting to centre-back six years ago. All Wolfsburg team captains wore rainbow armbands in the 2018-19 season, inspired by her lead, as part of the club's fight against discrimination.

CAROLINE SEGER
Born: 19 March 1985
Position: Midfielder

Inspirational leader in the centre of the park, she has been captain since 2009. Made the FIFA Women's World Cup All-star team in 2011, the UEFA Women's EURO team of the tournament in 2013 and is approaching a landmark 200 appearances. Has played in the USA and France, at Paris Saint-Germain as well as Olympique Lyonnais, with whom she won a treble of trophies that included the European title in 2016-17. She returned to Sweden in 2017, winning more silverware with FC Rosengård.

FRIDOLINA ROLFÖ
Born: 24 November 1993
Position: Forward

Along with *Blågult* defenders Jonna Andersson and Magdalena Eriksson, both now at Chelsea, she was part of Sweden's triumphant 2012 UEFA European Women's Under-19 Championship team and Linköpings FC's unbeaten 2016 *Damallsvenskan* winning side. Signed for Bayern Munich in 2016 and scored nine goals in 2017-18 on the way to a second successive *Frauen-Bundesliga* runners-up spot. An exciting, strong-running, left-footed forward, "Frido" can operate across the frontline or as a target player.

Above: Stalwart captain Caroline Seger is a crucial cog for Sweden.

WOMEN'S WORLD CUP RECORD

Year	Venue	Result
1991	China PR	Third place
1995	Sweden	Quarter-finalists
1999	USA	Quarter-finalists
2003	USA	Runners-up
2007	China PR	Group stage (3rd, Group B)
2011	Germany	Third place
2015	Canada	Round of 16

demonstrated their strength, quality and experience – goalkeeper Hedvig Lindahl, defenders Linda Sembrant and Nilla Fischer and midfielders Caroline Seger and Asllani all have over 100 caps – and performed under pressure, when it counted.

Iconic striker Lotta Schelin, who scored 88 times in 185 international appearances over 14 years and starred for Olympique Lyonnais, sadly retired in August 2018 due to chronic head and neck pain. Perhaps a young forward talent like Stina Blackstenius, Mimmi Larsson, Fridolina Rolfö or Olivia Schough will step into the limelight to become Sweden's new goalscoring heroine at France 2019.

FIFA WOMEN'S WORLD CUP™ RECORDS

Records are there to be broken, but some are tougher than others. The individual achievements of USA legend Michelle Akers and Swedish stalwart Lena Videkull in the inaugural FIFA Women's World Cup™ are yet to be bettered, while Canada 2015 saw several records smashed, particularly in the pulsating final between the USA and Japan. From champions to debutants, superstars to substitutes, young and old all have a chance to write themselves into the history books.

Main: Carli Lloyd's (10) 13-minute hat-trick against Japan at the FIFA Women's World Cup 2015 was the first in a final and helped the USA to once more become the overall top scorers in the competition's history, reclaiming the record from Germany.

FIFA WOMEN'S WORLD CUP™ TEAM RECORDS

Kicking off

Having tested the water in 1988 with an International Women's Football Tournament in China, FIFA organised their first official Women's World Championship in the same country three years later. Twelve teams qualified from the six continental confederations (only one each from Africa, Oceania, North America and South America), matches were just 80 minutes long and only two points were awarded for a win. Most crucially, as it turned out, the law aimed at discouraging backpasses had yet to be introduced. With the 1991 final finely poised at 1-1, Norway defender Tina Svensson's attempted backpass fell into the path of USA striker Michelle Akers in the dying minutes. Slotting home her tenth goal of the tournament and second of the match, in front of well over 60,000 spectators, Akers wrote her name into the history books as the USA won their first world title.

FIFA WOMEN'S WORLD CUP FINALS TOURNAMENTS

Year	Host nation	No. of venues	No. of teams	No. of matches	No. of goals	Average no. of goals per match
1991	China PR	6	12	26	99	3.8
1995	Sweden	5	12	26	99	3.8
1999	USA	8	16	32	123	3.8
2003	USA	6	16	32	107	3.3
2007	China PR	5	16	32	111	3.5
2011	Germany	9	16	32	86	2.7
2015	Canada	6	24	52	146	2.8

FIFA WOMEN'S WORLD CUP MEDAL MATCHES

Year	Host	Final	Match for third place
1991	China PR	USA 2-1 Norway	Sweden 4-0 Germany
1995	Sweden	Norway 2-0 Germany	USA 2-0 China PR
1999	USA	USA 0-0 *aet* China PR *USA won 5-4 on pens*	Brazil 0-0 Norway *Brazil won 5-4 on pens*
2003	USA	Germany 2-1 *aet* Sweden	USA 3-1 Canada
2007	China PR	Germany 2-0 Brazil	USA 4-1 Norway
2011	Germany	Japan 2-2 *aet* USA *Japan won 3-1 on pens*	Sweden 2-1 France
2015	Canada	USA 5-2 Japan	England 1-0 *aet* Germany

MEDAL TABLE

USA	7	3 gold, 1 silver, 3 bronze
Germany	3	2 gold, 1 silver
Sweden	3	1 silver, 2 bronze
Brazil	2	1 silver, 1 bronze
Japan	2	1 gold, 1 silver
Norway	2	1 gold, 1 silver
China PR	1	1 silver
England	1	1 bronze

Above: Michelle Akers' goal tally at the FIFA Women's World Cup 1991 will take some beating.

Above: *Twenty years after finishing rock bottom at the inaugural finals, the Nadeshiko were led to ultimate glory by captain Homare Sawa.*

Firsts at last

Before Japan stunned the USA in the 2011 final to become the first Asian side to lift a senior FIFA trophy, they had never beaten the Americans in 25 attempts. Four years later England finally broke the hoodoo that had seen them go 31 years without a single win over Germany when Fara Williams' extra-time penalty was enough to seal third place.

Champion of champions

Three-time champions USA have not only reached at least the semi-finals in every edition but have also never gone home empty-handed, earning a medal at every single finals tournament. Winners of the first Women's World Championship as well as the most recent, the USA also enjoyed an especially memorable victory on home soil in 1999, the final in Pasadena setting a FIFA Women's World Cup attendance record of 90,185 spectators at the Rose Bowl.

Chart toppers

Tournament top goalscorers twice before, Germany hit the heights once again at Canada 2015, helped in no small part by their 10-0 opener versus Côte d'Ivoire. A hat-trick apiece from Celia Šašić and Anja Mittag replicated the feat previously performed by Birgit Prinz and Sandra Smisek in Germany's record-smashing 11-0 victory over Argentina in 2007. Despite those efforts it was the USA who maintained their position as the most prolific goalscoring team, their five strikes in the final against Japan ensuring their overall tally of 112 pipped Germany's all-time FIFA Women's World Cup finals haul of 111.

HEARTBREAKERS

	Minute	Scorer
Latest golden goal	104'	Sissi (BRA) to finish off Nigeria who had battled back to 3-3 after being three goals down at half-time in the 1999 quarter-final.
Last golden goal	98'	Nia Künzer (GER) to beat Sweden in the 2003 final.
Latest goal in a knockout match	120'+2	Abby Wambach (USA) to equalise against Brazil in the 2011 quarter-final.
Latest normal-time winner	90'+2	Own goal from Laura Bassett (ENG) to give Japan a semi-final victory in 2015.

EVER-PRESENT TEAMS 1991–2015

Africa
Nigeria

Asia
Japan

Europe
Germany, Norway, Sweden

North America
USA

South America
Brazil

FIFA WOMEN'S WORLD CUP HIGHEST-SCORING TEAMS

Year	Team	Goals
1991	USA	25
1995	Norway	23
1999	China PR	19
2003	Germany	25
2007	Germany	21
2011	USA	13
2015	Germany	20

LONGEST RUNS

	No. of matches	Team	Editions
Longest winning run	10	Norway	1995-1999
Longest unbeaten run	15	Germany	2003-2011
Longest scoring run	15	Norway	1991–1999
Longest run without conceding	6	Germany	2007
Longest run without a win	12	New Zealand	1991, 2007-2015

FIFA WOMEN'S WORLD CUP™ PLAYER RECORDS

Above: 2015 adidas Golden Ball winner Carli Lloyd of the USA.

Trophy cabinet

For the last five editions the player of the tournament has also scored the most goals but 2015 adidas Golden Ball winner Carli Lloyd did not win the adidas Golden Boot after tying with Celia Šašić on goals and assists. Having played every second of the USA's title-winning run the midfielder lost out when time on the pitch was used as the final tiebreaker, the German striker having scored her six goals in a shorter amount of time. Lloyd was soon able to add to her trophy collection though when crowned FIFA Women's World Player of the Year 2015.

Ultimate hotshots

Nearly 12 years after opening her FIFA Women's World Cup account with a spot kick versus Korea Republic, Brazilian icon Marta finally clinched top spot in the scoring charts with her only goal at Canada 2015, a penalty scored against the very same opponents. FIFA Women's Player of the Century Michelle Akers' 12 goals across three editions included an incredible five-goal haul in the USA's 1991 7-0 quarter-final victory over Chinese Taipei. This feat remains unbeaten, along with her record for the most goals in a single tournament.

FIFA WOMEN'S WORLD CUP ADIDAS GOLDEN BALL AWARD

Year	adidas Golden Ball	adidas Silver Ball	adidas Bronze Ball
1991	Carin Jennings (USA)	Michelle Akers (USA)	Linda Medalen (NOR)
1995	Hege Riise (NOR)	Gro Espeseth (NOR)	Ann Kristin Aarønes (NOR)
1999	Sun Wen (CHN)	Sissi (BRA)	Michelle Akers (USA)
2003	Birgit Prinz (GER)	Victoria Svensson (SWE)	Maren Meinert (GER)
2007	Marta (BRA)	Birgit Prinz (GER)	Cristiane (BRA)
2011	Homare Sawa (JPN)	Abby Wambach (USA)	Hope Solo (USA)
2015	Carli Lloyd (USA)	Amandine Henry (FRA)	Aya Miyama (JPN)

ALL-TIME TOP SCORERS

	Goals	Tournament appearances
Marta (BRA)	15	2003, 2007, 2011, 2015
Birgit Prinz (GER)	14	1995, 1999, 2003, 2007, 2011
Abby Wambach (USA)	14	2003, 2007, 2011, 2015
Michelle Akers (USA)	12	1991, 1995, 1999
Sun Wen (CHN)	11	1991, 1995, 1999, 2003
Bettina Wiegmann (GER)	11	1991, 1995, 1999, 2003
Ann Kristin Aarønes (NOR)	10	1995, 1999
Heidi Mohr (GER)	10	1991, 1995

Right: Marta will be looking to extend her lead in the all-time top scorer charts in 2019.

Safe hands

Silke Rottenberg in 2003 and Nadine Angerer in 2007 were the first two recipients of the award for the tournament's best goalkeeper. Record-breaking Angerer did not concede a single goal at China 2007, even saving a penalty from Marta in the final against Brazil as Germany became the only team to date to retain the FIFA Women's World Cup.

High-speed records

USA 1999 saw two speedy records set as Australian teenager Alicia Ferguson was sent off in the second minute against China PR and Korea DPR's Ri Hyang Ok was cautioned in under a minute against Nigeria. After playing in two finals tournaments Ri returned to the world stage with her own set of cards to referee at Canada 2015.

Although the record for the quickest goal has not been broken since Lena Videkull scored for Sweden just 30 seconds into their match against Japan in the very first edition, the earliest hat-trick in a match was registered in 2015 when Carli Lloyd netted three in the first 16 minutes of the USA's final victory over Japan. The fastest hat-trick from first goal to last was also clocked in Canada, Fabienne Humm bagging a treble in just five minutes in the second half of Switzerland's 10-1 victory over Ecuador.

Above: Germany's Nadine Angerer reacts to saving Marta's penalty in the final – she just could not be beaten in 2007.

FIFA WOMEN'S WORLD CUP ADIDAS GOLDEN GLOVE AWARD

Year	Winner
2003	Silke Rottenberg (GER)
2007	Nadine Angerer (GER)
2011	Hope Solo (USA)
2015	Hope Solo (USA)

FIFA WOMEN'S WORLD CUP ADIDAS GOLDEN BOOT AWARD

Year	Winner	Goals
1991	Michelle Akers (USA)	10
1995	Ann Kristin Aarønes (NOR)	6
1999	Sissi (BRA); Sun Wen (CHN)	7
2003	Birgit Prinz (GER)	7
2007	Marta (BRA)	7
2011	Homare Sawa (JPN)	5
2015	Celia Šašić (GER)	6

OLD HEADS AND YOUNG SHOULDERS

Youngest player to play at a finals
Ifeanyi Chiejine (NGA), 16 years, 34 days
versus Korea DPR in 1999

Youngest player to score at a finals
Elena Danilova (RUS), 16 years, 107 days
versus Germany in 2003

Oldest player to play at a finals
Christie Rampone (USA), 40 years, 11 days
versus Japan in 2015

Oldest player to score at a finals
Formiga (BRA), 37 years, 98 days
versus Korea Republic in 2015

FIFA WOMEN'S WORLD CUP APPEARANCE RECORDS

Most finals attended	6
Formiga (BRA); Homare Sawa (JPN)	
Most matches played	30
Kristine Lilly (USA)	
Most medal-winning finishes	5
Kristine Lilly (USA); Christie Rampone (USA)	
Most appearances in the final	3
Birgit Prinz (GER)	

MATCH SCHEDULE

Watch the games, fill in the scores and follow the unfolding drama and excitement of the FIFA Women's World Cup France 2019™.

GROUP A

7 JUNE	21:00	PARIS			
FRANCE		**KOREA REPUBLIC**			
8 JUNE	21:00	REIMS			
NORWAY		**NIGERIA**			
12 JUNE	15:00	GRENOBLE			
NIGERIA		**KOREA REPUBLIC**			
12 JUNE	21:00	NICE			
FRANCE		**NORWAY**			
17 JUNE	21:00	RENNES			
NIGERIA		**FRANCE**			
17 JUNE	21:00	REIMS			
KOREA REPUBLIC		**NORWAY**			

TEAM	P	W	D	L	GD	PTS

GROUP B

8 JUNE	18:00	LE HAVRE			
SPAIN		**SOUTH AFRICA**			
8 JUNE	15:00	RENNES			
GERMANY		**CHINA PR**			
12 JUNE	18:00	VALENCIENNES			
GERMANY		**SPAIN**			
13 JUNE	21:00	PARIS			
SOUTH AFRICA		**CHINA PR**			
17 JUNE	18:00	MONTPELLIER			
SOUTH AFRICA		**GERMANY**			
17 JUNE	18:00	LE HAVRE			
CHINA PR		**SPAIN**			

TEAM	P	W	D	L	GD	PTS

GROUP C

9 JUNE	13:00	VALENCIENNES			
AUSTRALIA		**ITALY**			
9 JUNE	15:30	GRENOBLE			
BRAZIL		**JAMAICA**			
13 JUNE	18:00	MONTPELLIER			
AUSTRALIA		**BRAZIL**			
14 JUNE	18:00	REIMS			
JAMAICA		**ITALY**			
18 JUNE	21:00	GRENOBLE			
JAMAICA		**AUSTRALIA**			
18 JUNE	21:00	VALENCIENNES			
ITALY		**BRAZIL**			

TEAM	P	W	D	L	GD	PTS

GROUP D

9 JUNE	18:00	NICE			
ENGLAND		**SCOTLAND**			
10 JUNE	18:00	PARIS			
ARGENTINA		**JAPAN**			
14 JUNE	15:00	RENNES			
JAPAN		**SCOTLAND**			
14 JUNE	21:00	LE HAVRE			
ENGLAND		**ARGENTINA**			
19 JUNE	21:00	NICE			
JAPAN		**ENGLAND**			
19 JUNE	21:00	PARIS			
SCOTLAND		**ARGENTINA**			

TEAM	P	W	D	L	GD	PTS

GROUP E

10 JUNE **CANADA**	21:00	MONTPELLIER **CAMEROON**	
11 JUNE **NEW ZEALAND**	15:00	LE HAVRE **THE NETHERLANDS**	
15 JUNE **THE NETHERLANDS**	15:00	VALENCIENNES **CAMEROON**	
15 JUNE **CANADA**	21:00	GRENOBLE **NEW ZEALAND**	
20 JUNE **THE NETHERLANDS**	18:00	REIMS **CANADA**	
20 JUNE **CAMEROON**	18:00	MONTPELLIER **NEW ZEALAND**	

TEAM	P	W	D	L	GD	PTS

GROUP F

11 JUNE **CHILE**	18:00	RENNES **SWEDEN**	
11 JUNE **USA**	21:00	REIMS **THAILAND**	
16 JUNE **USA**	18:00	PARIS **CHILE**	
16 JUNE **SWEDEN**	15:00	NICE **THAILAND**	
20 JUNE **SWEDEN**	21:00	LE HAVRE **USA**	
20 JUNE **THAILAND**	21:00	RENNES **CHILE**	

TEAM	P	W	D	L	GD	PTS

ROUND OF 16

(37) 22 JUNE	21:00	NICE	
2A			**2C**

(38) 22 JUNE	17:30	GRENOBLE	
1B			**3ACD**

(39) 23 JUNE	17:30	VALENCIENNES	
1D			**3BEF**

(40) 23 JUNE	21:00	LE HAVRE	
1A			**3CDE**

(41) 24 JUNE	18:00	REIMS	
2B			**1F**

(42) 24 JUNE	21:00	PARIS	
2F			**2E**

(43) 25 JUNE	18:00	MONTPELLIER	
1C			**3ABF**

(44) 25 JUNE	21:00	RENNES	
1E			**2D**

QUARTER-FINALS

(45) 27 JUNE	21:00	LE HAVRE	
W37			**W39**

(46) 28 JUNE	21:00	PARIS	
W40			**W41**

(47) 29 JUNE	15:00	VALENCIENNES	
W43			**W44**

(48) 29 JUNE	18:30	RENNES	
W38			**W42**

SEMI-FINALS

(49) 2 JULY	21:00	LYON	
W45			**W46**

(50) 3 JULY	21:00	LYON	
W47			**W48**

MATCH FOR THIRD PLACE

(51) 6 JULY	17:00	NICE	
RU49			**RU50**

FINAL

(52) 7 JULY	17:00	LYON	
W49			**W50**

ALL TIMES ARE LOCAL.
SEE PAGE 96 FOR EXPLANATION OF THE MATCH SCHEDULE.

CREDITS

AUTHORS' ACKNOWLEDGEMENTS

In the process of compiling this book we were afforded generous assistance from the following people who are reporters and supporters of the women's game: Janine Anthony, Sven Beyrich, Nick Cavell, Carolina Garcia and Ann Odong. We would also particularly like to thank the following association and federation websites and individuals for quotes used: FIFA.com; the-afc.com; football.no; svenskfotboll.se; uefa.com; Christian Brookes; and Kieran Theivam.

PICTURE CREDITS

The publishers would like to thank the following sources for their kind permission to reproduce the pictures in this book. Key: T=top, B=bottom, L=left, R=right.

GETTY IMAGES: 65; /Luis Acosta/AFP: 64TR; /Action Foto Sport/NurPhoto: 57, 60BR, 70TL; /Samuel Ahmadu/Gallo Images: 36BL, 46BR; /Robin Alam/Icon Sportswire: 42TL, 42BR, 51, 55; /Emilio Andreoli: 53; /Adek Berry/AFP: 32TL; /Manuel Blondeau/Icon Sport: 58-59, 86BL; /Thomas Bregardis/Icon Sport: 24; /Sean Burges/Icon Sportswire: 71; /Robert Cianflone: 50BR; /Jean-Pierre Clatot/AFP: 72BL; /Kevin C Cox: 26-27, 88-89; /Elsa: 80BL; /Dominique Faget/AFP: 8-9; /Gualter Fatia: 80TR; /Tony Feder: 50BL; /Franck Fife/AFP: 31; /George Frey: 40BL; /Alex Grimm/FIFA: 10, 45; /Dennis Grombkowski: 92TL; /Jack Guez/AFP: 66TL; /Martyn Harrison/AFP: 18-19; /Alexander Hassenstein/FIFA: 4, 17; /Karina Hessland-Wissel/Bongarts: 40TR; /Hagen Hopkins: 74TL; /Harry How: 47; /Gilbert Iundt/Corbis: 90; /Gerard Julien/AFP: 28-29; /Steven Kingsman/Icon Sports Wire: 20; /Romain Lafabregue/Icon Sport: 30BL; /Xavier Laine: 78-79; /Pascal Le Segretain/FIFA: 36BR, 72BR; /MacGregor/Topical Press Agency/Hulton Archive: 22; /Gabriele Maltini: 52TL, 52BR; /Ludovic Marin/AFP: 96; /Ronald Martinez: 12; /Stephen McCarthy/Sportsfile: 35; /Patrick McDermott: 25; /Aurelien Meunier/FIFA: 16; /Vincent Michel/Icon Sport: 30TR, 70BR; /Daniel Mihailescu/AFP: 44BL; /Jeff J Mitchell: 62BL; /Christopher Morris/Corbis: 73; /Dean Mouhtaropoulos: 6-7, 46BL; /Dan Mullan: 61; /Nathan Munkley/Action Plus: 60BL; /Francois Nel: 33, 43, 66BR, 67; /Guang Niu: 93; /Doug Pensinger: 21; /Joe Petro/Icon Sportswire: 74BR; /Stephen Pond: 56BL; /Anne-Christine Poujoulat/AFP: 68-69; /Adam Pretty/FIFA: 37; /Quality Sport Images: 44TR, 75; /Mark Ralston/AFP: 92BR; /Claudio Reyes/AFP: 54TR, 84TR; /Andre Ringuette: 32BR, 82BL; /Lars Ronbog/FrontZoneSport: 86TR; /Martin Rose/FIFA: 64BL; /Will Russell: 83; /Thomas Samson/AFP: 11; /Tim Sloan/AFP: 23; /Soccrates: 76BL; /Trond Tandberg: 34TL; /Team 2 Sportphoto/ullstein bild: 91; /Jean Paul Thomas/Icon Sport: 48-49; /Charly Triballeau/AFP: 38-39, 84BL, 85; /Nicolas Tucat/AFP: 87; /VI Images: 34BR, 41; /Omar Vega: 56BR; /Eric Verhoeven/Soccrates: 13, 76TR, 77; /Matthew Visinsky/Icon Sportswire: 81; /Scott Winters/Icon Sportswire: 54BL; /David Woodley/Action Plus: 82BR

THE SCOTTISH FA: 62TR

SHUTTERSTOCK: /Craig Doyle/Prosports/REX: 63

Every effort has been made to acknowledge correctly and contact the source and/or copyright holder of each picture and Carlton Books Limited apologises for any unintentional errors or omissions that will be corrected in future editions of this book.

KEY NOTES FOR THE MATCH SCHEDULE (PP94–95)

Notes for deciding the group stages

P = played (each team plays three group matches); W = win; D = draw; L = loss; F = goals scored (for); A = goals conceded (against); Pts = points. Three points for a win; one for a draw; no points for a loss.

After most points, groups are decided first by better positive goal difference, then total goals scored. After this, the head-to-head results will decide the order, and if three teams are involved, it is again goal difference in these matches, then goals scored. After this, fair play points in group matches will be counted, with the team with the highest score progressing. If teams are still equal, then the FIFA Organising Committee will draw lots.

Explanation of knockout stage

All knockout matches will be decided on the day. If the scores are level after 90 minutes, extra time (two 15-minute periods) will be played. If the scores remain level, kicks from the penalty mark (penalty shoot-out) will decide the winner. Teams will take five kicks, alternately, unless one team cannot win after three or four attempts. If the scores are still level after 10 attempts, then a sudden-death shoot-out follows, decided by one team scoring and the other failing.

The alpha-numeric designations in the second round refer to first-round group positions. 1A is the winner of Group A, 2F is the runner-up in Group F. The four third-placed teams with the best records in the first round will join the group winners and runners-up. The third-placed teams will play the winner of a group other than the one in which they have already played.

The match numbers are the official tournament match numbers and W before the number refers to the winners of that tie (RU denotes runner-up), thus the first semi-final, match 49, will be between the winners of quarter-final matches 45 and 46.